Mick Donovan

youth basketball
drills

Note
Whilst every effort has been made to ensure that the content of this book is as technically accurate and as sound as possible, neither the author nor the publishers can accept responsibility for any injury or loss sustained as a result of the use of this material.

Published by
A & C Black Publishers Ltd
36 Soho Square
London W1D 3QY
www.acblack.com

ISBN 978 14081 2954 8

A CIP catalogue record for this book is available from the British Library.

Acknowledgements
Cover photograph by Tom Croft
Inside photographs by Tom Croft, except pp 16, 36, 54, 76, 86 © Getty Images
Illustrations by Mark Silver
Designed by James Watson
Commissioned by Charlotte Croft
Edited by Kate Turvey

This book is produced using paper that is made from wood grown in managed, sustainable forests. It is natural, renewable and recyclable. The logging and manufacturing processes conform to the environmental regulations of the country of origin.

Typeset in 10 on 12pt Din Regular by Margaret Brain, Wisbech

Printed and bound in the UK by Martins the Printers

CONTENTS

ABOUT THE AUTHOR

Within his current role as the Head of Institute of Sports and Exercise Science at the University of Worcester, Mick has pioneered the new MSc degree in European Basketball Coaching Science, in collaboration with the Lithuanian Basketball Federation – a course which is attracting coaches from around the world. The University of Worcester men's team have been crowned British Universities & Colleges Sport champions four times since 2003 and have represented the UK in European and World University events. Mick created the Worcester 'study and play basketball programme' and each year the University receive hundreds of applications to study in areas related to playing, coaching and development.

Mick currently holds Senior Coach status within England Basketball. His most notable achievements in recent years include the creation of the Worcester Wolves Basketball Club in 2000 and leading the coach education programme for performance and recreation/community coaches. Mick was also one of the creators of the 'Learning Through Sport' initiative which includes a basketball element in attempting to improve Maths and English ability in key stage 2 children.

Before entering Higher Education, Mick enjoyed a thirteen-year career as a PE teacher in secondary schools in Manchester, Athens and the Midlands. He achieved significant success with young players in terms of increasing basketball participation at recreational level, and within English and European Schools championships.

ACKNOWLEDGEMENTS

I would like to thank a number of people who have played their part in supporting me during the compilation of this book: April White, for giving her time and expertise in formatting all of the drills; and the coaches Mindaugas Balciunas, Paul James and Guy Evans who offered ideas off court and inspiration on it. Particular thanks go to Harvey Smith and Emma Fitzpatrick who managed to bring the drills to life with the initial sketches. Thanks also to Glyn Harding, for sharing his thoughts and experiences and confirming through endless debates that the same drills can be adapted to many sports. Finally, to my three girls: Liz, my wife and daughters Katie and Megan who have always shown patience and support when the basketball stories and sagas have unfolded, regardless of the outcome.

FOREWORD

Mick and I have only known each other for a relatively short time, however, during this period, I have learnt a great deal about his 'Learning Through Sport' philosophy that encourages players and coaches to think for themselves. Since I have been involved in the Worcester programme, I can see that he has drawn upon his extensive experience as a coach and an educator to create a vision that will enhance the development of many types of people in basketball-related areas.

Within the sporting environment, we need to continue to produce coaches who can focus on developing players capable of making decisions and who are eager to improve their own performance at all levels. *101 Youth Basketball Drills* is an essential resource for both teachers and coaches who are new to the sport, and for the more experienced practitioners who are looking for new ideas when challenging their players.

Paul James
Head Coach: England Basketball Senior Men's team
Head Coach: Worcester Wolves, British Basketball League

KEY TO DIAGRAMS

- - - - - - - - - - - - - - ->   Direction of pass

───────────────►   Direction of moving player

∿∿∿∿►   Dribble

△ △ △   Cones

- - - - - - - - - - - - -   Imaginary line dividing court

KEY TERMS

Assist: the last pass to a teammate that leads directly to a basket being scored; the scorer must move immediately towards the basket for the passer to be credited with an assist; only one assist can be credited per field goal.

Backboard: the rectangular structure to which the basket is attached.

Backcourt: the area from the middle of the court to the baseline, the defensive end of the court.

Baseline: the area line behind each basket.

Basket: attached to the backboard, it consists of a metal ring 18 inches in diameter suspended 10 feet from the floor, from which a net hangs.

Beat the defender: when an offensive player, with or without the ball, is able to get past an opponent.

Blocking out: a player's attempt to position his body between his opponents and the basket to assist with rebounding.

Centre circle: the marked circle in the middle of the court from which jump balls are taken.

Charging: an offensive foul that occurs when an offensive player runs into a defender who already has established a set position.

Court vision: a player's ability to see everything on the court during play, such as where his teammates and defenders are positioned, and which enables him to make appropriate decisions.

Crossover dribble: when a player dribbles the ball across his body from one hand to the other.

Defence: the act of preventing the offence from scoring; the team without the ball.

Defensive rebound: a rebound of an opponent's missed shot.

Dribbling: when a player repeatedly pushes the ball towards the floor with one hand to cause the ball to bounce back up to either of his hands; used to move with the ball and keep it under control.

Drive to the basket: to move quickly towards the basket with the ball.

Fake: a deceptive move to throw a defender off-balance and allow an offensive player to shoot or make a pass; players use their eyes, head or any other part of the body to 'fake' an opponent or pretend to shoot.

Fast break: begins with a defensive rebound by a player who immediately sends an outlet pass towards the halfway line to his waiting teammates, who then break towards the offensive basket before the opponent can react.

Forwards: two of the bigger players on the team who play nearer to the basket.

Free-throw: an unguarded shot taken from the line by a player who has been fouled.

Guarding: the act of following an opponent around the court to prevent him from getting close to the basket, taking an open shot or making a pass.

Guards: the two players on each team who are the smallest on the court; they are normally responsible for outside shooting, setting up plays and passing to teammates closer to the basket.

Inside shooting: shots taken by a player near the basket.

Jump ball: two opposing players jump for the ball after the referee flips the ball above and between them, to tip it to their teammates and gain possession. It is used to start the game.

Lay-up: a shot taken after driving to the basket, taking two steps and using one hand to push the ball off the backboard.

Lead pass: when a passer throws the ball in the direction he thinks a receiver is moving.

Loose ball: a ball that is live but not in the possession of either team.

Man-to-man defence: where each defensive player is responsible for marking one opponent.

Match-ups: any pairing of players on opposing teams who mark each other.

Offence: the team with possession of the ball.

Offensive rebound: a rebound of a team's own missed shot.

Open: when an offensive player is unguarded by a defender.

Out of bounds: the area outside of the baselines and sidelines.

Outside shooting: shots taken from outside the zone.

Pass: when a player throws the ball to a teammate, used to start plays or to keep the ball away from defenders.

Personal foul: contact between players that may provide one team with an unfair advantage, players may not push, hold, trip, elbow etc.

Pivot: after stopping with the ball, pivoting allows the player to change direction and look for a pass or shot. The player must not move the foot they stopped on.

Possession: to be holding or in control of the ball.

Rebound: when a player grabs a ball that is coming off the ring or backboard after a shot attempt. This can be in the form of an offensive or defensive rebound.

Receiver: the player who receives a pass from a teammate.

Screen: the offensive player who stands between a teammate and a defender to create space and time for his teammate to take an open shot or to get free.

Shooter: a player who shoots at the basket.

Sidelines: the two boundary lines that run the length of the court.

Three-point shot: a scored shot worth three points because the shooter releases the ball behind the three-point line.

Timeout: the time taken during a game by the coach to speak with the players.

Tip-off: the initial jump ball that starts the game.

Travelling: a violation, when a player takes too many steps without dribbling.

Triple threat: a position taken by an offensive player upon receiving the ball. The player should pivot to face the basket and position the body so that the options of shooting, passing or dribbling are viable.

Violation: a player's action that violates the rules but does not prevent an opponent's movement or cause him harm. Results in the team losing the ball.

Zone: the area near the basket bordered by the end line and the free throw line, also the area in which an offensive player cannot spend more than three seconds at any time.

Zone defence: a defensive strategy, where each defender is responsible for an area of the court and must mark any player who enters that area.

INTRODUCTION

Most physical education teachers and coaches have grown up in a competitive environment and have experienced the positive and negative effects of competition. Those teachers and coaches who promote competition must ensure that it is delivered in a structured way. For those children who do not respond to competition, another route has to be taken that will offer everybody the opportunity to succeed.

Since moving into higher education I have been given several opportunities to reflect on the methods I have used as a PE teacher and a coach, and have been able to research various other current methods and philosophies. Some coaches prefer to direct or guide their young players rather than help them to discover; indeed, one coach questioned why he would spend two weeks helping a player to discover a skill when he could direct him to learn a point in one hour. The answer is that by learning for themselves, the young players will develop a better understanding that will serve them well in later years in a range of sporting activities and social situations. Whilst the purpose of this book is not to debate different coaching styles in any detail I do believe that coaches and teachers should be aware of the many approaches that exist. There is often a healthy and productive compromise that will aid learning and understanding for their players.

The coach or teacher has to be aware of both the negative and positive impacts of competition. Whilst many supporters of team games and competition frequently claim that this encourages discipline, loyalty, commitment and cooperation, others warn of selfish individuals, ruthless competitivism and of a sense of failure after being involved in a competitive sport. I am a great believer in the importance of competition, yet youngsters can be 'crushed' by poorly prepared sessions. The coach or the teacher must limit bad experiences and make sure the sessions are positive for all participants. Hopefully, the 101 drills in this book will help achieve this. I hope that you enjoy the book and I encourage you to remind players and coaches of our philosophy at Worcester:

Attitude affects Outcome

SESSION GUIDELINES

The effective coach will often list safety, fun and learning as essential when planning sessions. All three are crucial, yet most young players enjoy sport more if they feel that they are safe and that they are improving. Fun on its own can sometimes be dangerous and will not engage youngsters in the longer term.

Planning for progression

When planning coaching sessions it is important to be aware of the current ability range of the group and there should be the opportunity for all participants to succeed. Hopefully, the coach and the players understand that players will have to make decisions for themselves in game situations and waiting to be told what to do in game situations can limit progression for individual players and the team. The coach should include opportunities for decision making and practising skills, whilst providing challenges that are related to a game situation. Children are learning when they ask meaningful questions and provide thoughtful answers.

Session content

The coach should always be striving to introduce varied practices and drills. Players will disengage through boredom and too much repetition of drills. In my experience, seven to ten minutes is an adequate time to spend on one particular drill. If the coach is not happy with the progress made in that time, then it is possible to continue with the same learning focus with a different drill. How often have we heard a coach say 'we are not leaving this gym until we get this right'? A more creative approach, whilst still staying on task is the key. Often, the most realistic targets can be set by the players themselves and it is important to reflect with them about the progress they have made and their future aims. Within this book there are many isolated skills practices, and many game-related small-sided games (one versus one, two versus one, two versus three, three versus three etc.) that will offer realistic progression for the learner.

Equipment and organisation

Many of the drills require the players to have a ball each and just as it is difficult for children to learn to write effectively when sharing a pencil with another class mate, it is equally frustrating for young players to wait for a turn when they could be learning with a ball of their own. If this is not possible, then alternative yet meaningful tasks need to be set for the young players while they wait and watch their peers.

Basketballs and cones

The coach should ensure that there is at least one ball to every player and if the school does not have extensive resources, it is worth remembering that footballs and netballs are the same size as mini basketballs and can be used instead. Furthermore, the players will not all be the same height or have the same sized hands, and they clearly will not have the same physical strength; therefore the coach should provide a variety of ball sizes.

Whilst flat cones are ideal to mark out practice areas, taller cones are more appropriate when being used as defenders and will discourage the player from walking or dribbling through them; which would not happen against a defender.

Court and rings

The court markings in the diagram on page 4 show there is great potential to set players tasks in specific areas that are already signposted (three point line, zone, centre circle, mid-court etc.). In most secondary schools there are baskets and backboards on the sideline of the court which encourages smaller groups to engage in shooting practices. However, the coach should also consider using a range of different tasks if there are restricted resources. For example, whilst some of the group are shooting, others could practise dribbling and passing in the mid court.

Many primary schools do not have a basketball court and whilst many of the practices do not necessarily need a basketball ring, the young players will always want to score a basket. The alternatives are mobile rings that can be stored away in a box, or a netball ring in the playground or the assembly hall. Many of the schools that our club visits have benefitted from government sports grants to purchase mobile equipment. Some feeder primary schools have also developed partnerships with secondary schools that involve sharing facilities.

WARM-UPS AND BALL HANDLING

The warm-up should be used in a meaningful way to prepare the body and mind for the game or practice to come.

Whenever possible, the warm-up should not be done in isolation from the activities that are to follow and the players should use the opportunity to improve skills and technique (footwork, passing, dribbling etc.) whilst getting ready to play. I have included ball handling in this section, because it is vital that when the players go into a game or practice that they are familiar and feel comfortable with the shape and the weight of the ball.

During the warm-up, the players should also be challenged to make some decisions and be encouraged to concentrate so that they are alert and ready to make progress.

drill 1 court familiarity

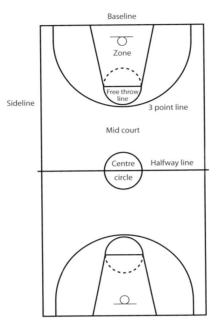

Objective: To warm up the body and improve listening skills and defensive footwork within the different areas of the court. This drill will enable beginners to learn about the significance of court markings and allows the coach to introduce fundamental rules.

Equipment: Full court.

Description: Distribute the players evenly around the outside of the court. The coach shouts 'jog' and the players jog in a clockwise direction around the outside of the court. The coach shouts 'out' and the players move into a defensive stance position taking 'step, slide' movements (see drill 3, defensive slides) in the same direction facing the outside of the court. The coach shouts 'in' and the players go in the same direction, but turn and face the inside of the court. The coach shouts the name of a part of the court and the players run to the nearest correct location and stutter (moving both feet alternately and rapidly) on the spot. The coach then shouts 'sideline' and the players run back to the outside of the court and jog in the opposite direction, awaiting new instructions.

Coaching points: Encourage the players to maintain correct body posture whilst moving in a defensive sidestep motion (see section on defensive play for clear guidelines).

Progression: With more experienced players, the drill can be performed at game-speed which will recreate the intensity of defending an opponent.

drill 2 ski jumps

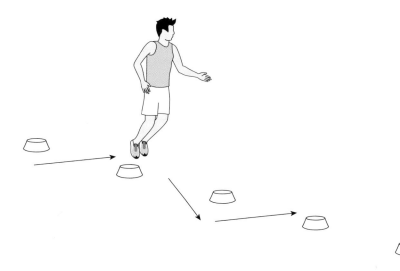

Objective: To warm up the body and improve balance and coordination.

Equipment: Players, cones and half the court.

Description: Six cones are placed in a line at one metre intervals with the players lined up at one end. With their feet together, the players bounce on the balls of their feet and move forwards in a zig-zag direction in and out of the cones. Players can vary the number of bounces to suit their ability level.

Coaching points: Encourage the players to bend their knees and use their arms to assist with balance.

Progression: Experienced players can be given a target time to reach the end of the line, or can be asked to bounce higher to develop their jumping skills.

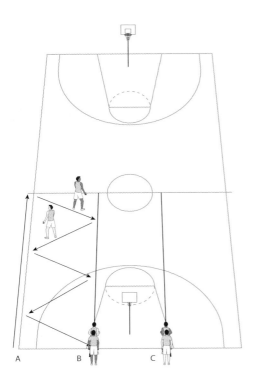

Objective: To warm up the body and develop defensive footwork.

Equipment: Players, cones and half of the court.

Description: The half court is divided into three lanes and in teams the players form lines on the baseline to the left side of each lane (A, B and C). At intervals, individual players jog to the halfway line and then use defensive 'step, slide' movements to return to the baseline. The players follow a zig-zag formation and face the halfway line at all times. The coach can also use the other half of the court when dealing with a large group. The drill should take ten minutes.

Coaching points: The players should be encouraged to maintain the correct defensive position and keep their heads and hands up, but with a lowered body position, throughout the drill. It is crucial that players do not cross their feet.

Progression: Introduce a partner with a ball who will dribble facing a defender while following the same route. Players change places after each journey.

drill 4 — warm-up: footwork and dodge

Objective: To improve footwork and speed when warming up the body.

Equipment: Two cones and two players.

Description: Two cones are placed 3 m apart on a line on the court. The two players face each other, either side of the line. One player takes on the role of attacker and the other takes up a defensive stance position. On the command of the coach, the attacking player uses a range of footwork moves to try to pass the defensive player before he is tagged by him. The players must stay within the boundaries of the cones.

Coaching points: The players stay low, on the balls of their feet and use a range of foot fakes and body fakes to create space.

Progression: Once the players have sound footwork, a ball can be used by the attacking player.

Objective: To develop ball handling skills and encourage basic stretching movements.

Equipment: One ball for each player.

Description: The player begins by holding the ball above the head with both hands, 'patting' (pushing quickly from hand to hand) the ball with both hands for a set time. The player then brings the ball down to the head level and rotates the ball around the head. The player then rotates the ball around the waist, the right ankle and then the left ankle. The ball can be at each station for forty-five seconds or ten rotations.

Coaching points: In the early stages, beginners will look at the ball but as the player becomes more familiar with the drill, they should be encouraged to keep their head in an upright position.

Progression: Once the players have moved the ball down the body, they can reverse the routine and move the ball back up towards the original starting position. Advanced players can use this drill before every practice and perform at a faster speed each time.

drill 6 figure of eight

Objective: To develop ball handling skills and encourage basic stretching skills.

Equipment: One ball for each player.

Description: The player stands with feet shoulder-width apart and bends down, holding the ball. They then make a figure of eight by passing the ball from hand to hand around the legs (without touching the floor). The player repeats this movement ten times.

Coaching points: In the early stages, beginners will look at the ball but as the player becomes more familiar with the drill, they should be encouraged to keep their head in an upright position.

Progression: The player can perform the same drill by moving the ball in different directions or while walking.

Objective: To develop ball handling and coordination skills.

Equipment: One ball for each player.

Description: The player stands with feet shoulder-width apart and holds the ball in both hands at waist height. The player feeds the ball into the air, claps their hands and catches the ball with both hands. As the player gets more confident, the ball is fed higher and the number of claps can be increased.

Coaching points: The players should watch and follow the path of the ball and absorb the ball when catching it rather than reaching to catch.

Progression: The player can feed the ball into the air and clap hands behind their back, between their legs or even going down on one knee to clap, before catching the ball. The drill can be developed into a competition as the players attempt to beat their own personal best score or the score of their teammates.

drill 8 — overhead feed and catch

Objective: To develop ball handling and coordination skills.

Equipment: One ball for each player.

Description: The player stands with their feet shoulder-width apart and holds the ball with both hands at waist height. The player feeds the ball into the air, claps their hands and catches the ball behind their back. As the player becomes more confident, the ball is fed higher and the number of claps can be increased.

Coaching points: Keep the back straight when attempting to catch the ball.

Progression: The player can feed the ball into the air and clap hands behind their back or between their legs before catching the ball behind their back.

Objective: To develop ball handling and coordination skills.

Equipment: One ball for each player.

Description: The player stands with feet shoulder-width apart. The ball is held in both hands with outstretched arms at waist height. The player must bounce the ball backwards and forwards between their legs, moving their hands accordingly to catch it to the back and front of the body.

Coaching points: At first, players should look towards the ball and be encouraged to bounce the ball at the central point on the floor, between their legs. Once a rhythm has been developed, the players will feed the ball harder and will not need to look down.

drill 10 over and under

Objective: To develop ball handling, coordination and communication skills.

Equipment: One ball between two players.

Description: Players stand back to back with feet shoulder-width apart. Player 1 starts with the ball in both hands at waist height and then passes the ball overhead to player 2 who has outstretched arms. Player 2 then passes the ball through their legs back to player 1. The process is repeated ten times and the players then change the direction of the ball. They should be encouraged to look ahead throughout the drill.

Coaching points: Both players should look to stretch when passing and receiving the ball, beginning slowly before establishing rhythm and team work.

Progression: Once warmed up, the experienced players can perform the drill at speed and attempt to beat their best time or race against other pairs.

drill 11 flip drill

Objective: To improve ball handling skills and coordination.

Equipment: One player and one ball.

Description: The player bends over with his feet shoulder-width apart, with both hands holding the ball behind their legs. They then flip the ball forwards, and between their legs and then quickly move their hands outside their legs to catch the ball in front of the body. The process is then repeated backwards and forwards.

Coaching points: When the ball is flipped in a slightly upward direction, the player will have more time to move their hands.

Progression: The experienced player can perform this drill at speed and attempt to beat their best time or race against other individuals.

drill 12 drops drill

Objective: To improve ball handling skills and coordination.

Equipment: One player and one ball.

Description: The player bends over with their feet shoulder-width apart, holding the ball between their lower legs with the right hand in front of the body and left hand behind the body. The player then attempts to swap the position of their hands (the right hand to the back of the body and left hand to the front of the body) and catch the ball before it touches the ground. This pattern continues for a set amount of time or for a target number of touches set by the coach.

Coaching points: When releasing the ball, it can be directed upwards slightly, which allows more time for the player to move their hands.

Progression: The experienced player can perform this drill at speed and attempt to beat their best time or race against other individuals.

Allen Iverson of the Memphis Grizzlies demonstrates that good technique and concentration are important when passing the ball.

PASSING

One of the greatest temptations for young players when they are first introduced to basketball is to bounce or dribble the ball. This is not always a bad thing, but it does discourage players from looking up to see other options that may include passing to a teammate who is in a better position. A key point is that a successful pass will normally enable the ball to reach the target faster than a dribbled ball. Players are faced with a range of challenges within a game situation and it is vital that they develop an understanding of the passing options that exist. Only when they make the correct decision will they execute an appropriate pass.

Types of pass
Chest pass

Bounce pass

Overhead pass

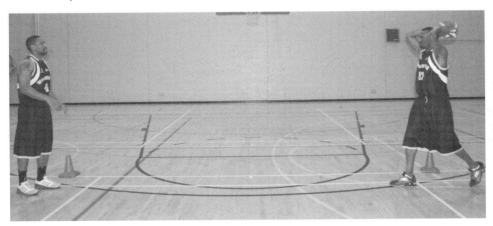

Javelin pass

Key principles to remember

Passing principles

■ The ball should be passed quickly to outwit the defender

■ The passer should protect and be in control of the ball before the pass

■ The weight of the passing player should be transferred from back foot to front foot, using the 'pivot' to step into the pass

■ The ball should be passed to the receiver's hands either directly or slightly ahead, but not behind

■ Upon release of the ball, follow through with arms, wrists and hands in the direction of the pass.

Receiving principles

■ Receivers should offer a target (one hand if moving, and two hands if stationary)

■ Move towards the pass and meet the ball before the defender intercepts

■ On receipt of the ball, in most cases, move into a triple threat position.

drill 13 three versus three 'get free'

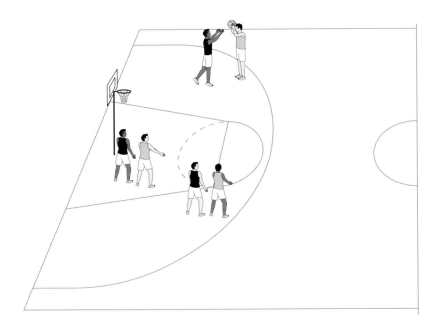

Objective: To improve passing technique and create space.

Equipment: Two teams of three players, one third of the court and one ball.

Description: This game can be played within the three point shooting arc or on a third of the court. There are two teams of three players. One team starts with the ball and the aim is to make as many passes as possible without the defenders blocking the ball. The teams change roles when the defending team intercepts the ball, or when 20 consecutive passes are made.

Coaching points: The players should be encouraged to use appropriate offensive footwork to find space and to make good passes. The emphasis of this drill can also be placed on improving defensive play.

drill 14 pass and move

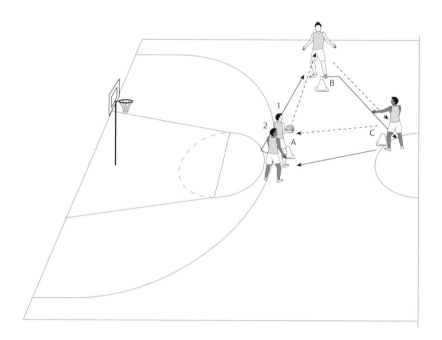

Objective: To encourage players to pass and move to create space.

Equipment: Four players, three cones and one ball.

Description: Cones are placed 5 m apart to form a triangle. Two players stand behind one cone (A) and one player behind each of the remaining cones (B and C). The first chest pass is made from the player standing at cone A towards the player who is placed at cone B; the passing player follows the pass. The receiving player then pivots and passes to the player at cone C and then follows the pass. Once 20 passes have been made, the direction and type of pass can be changed.

Coaching points: The players should be encouraged to signal for the ball when receiving a pass and use correct footwork throughout the drill when passing and receiving in order to avoid 'travelling' which is an illegal movement.

drill 15 pop-up pass

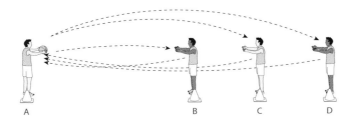

Objective: To enable beginners to pass the ball over a range of distances and develop spatial awareness.

Equipment: Four players, four cones and one ball.

Description: Four cones are placed in a straight line over a distance of 5 m. The distance from cone A to B is 3 m, from B to C is 1 m, and from C to D is 1 m. One player stands at each cone. Player A passes to B who returns the ball to player A before crouching down. Player A then passes the ball over player B to player C who returns the ball and crouches down. Player A then passes the ball to player D who remains standing and returns the ball to player A. Player A then passes the ball again to player D who returns the ball to player A. Player A then exchanges passes with player C who has returned to the standing position. Player A then exchanges passes with player B who has returned to a standing position. The players then change position.

Coaching points: The receiving player should be encouraged to signal for the ball. The passing player should step into the pass and follow through with their arms and hands on release.

Progression: Once beginners are confident, this drill can be used for relay races with large groups of players.

drill 16 pepper pot passing

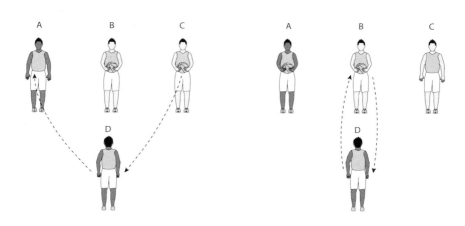

Objective: To develop confidence when passing and receiving in a pressurised situation.

Equipment: Four players and two balls.

Description: Three players (A, B and C) stand alongside each other, arm's length apart. Player D stands opposite player B (the central player), who is 5 m away. Players B and C hold the balls at the beginning of the drill. Player C will make a chest pass to player D who receives the ball and returns the pass to player A. Player B then passes to player D who returns the ball to player B. Player A then passes to player D who receives and passes to player C; player B passes to player D who returns the pass to player B. This sequence continues. Players must only pass when the receiving player signals for the ball to indicate that they are ready.

Coaching points: The coach should encourage players to step into the chest pass and follow through with outstretched arms and hands, and to signal for the ball when receiving the pass.

Progression: As the players become more confident, the speed of the passing can be increased.

Objective: To develop communication and speed of reaction when performing short passes.

Equipment: Two players, two balls and two cones.

Description: The players divide into pairs with a ball each, standing 5 m apart and facing each other. On a signal from the coach, both players will pass to each other at the same time with one player using a chest pass and one player a bounce pass. The aim will be to make 20 passes. Players then alternate the type of pass that they are using.

Coaching points: Emphasis should be placed on the importance of accurate and firm passing with good use of the pivot foot on delivery.

Progression: The coach can introduce a competition with races against other pairs, or set targets for the number of passes within a given time.

drill 18 pass and react

Objective: To develop passing skills and improve reaction skills and awareness.

Equipment: Six players and two balls.

Description: The players form a circle, arm's length apart and two of the players hold a ball. Players can then pass the ball to any other player. The main focus for the receiver is to watch the other members of the group and their actions. The main focus for the passer is to observe where other passes are going.

Coaching points: All players who receive the ball should look to pass quickly and safely and then have their hands in position, ready to receive the ball. If there is any doubt related to balls clashing, the players should delay the pass.

Progression: Once the players are confident, the speed of passing can be increased.

Objective: To improve passing, awareness and fitness.

Equipment: Eight players, cones and one ball.

Description: Four players form a circle, arm's length apart (cones can be used to help younger players to find the correct position); the remaining four players form an outer circle 2 m away. The players in the inner circle jog in a clockwise direction and the players in the outer circle jog in an anti-clockwise direction. The ball must be passed from one player in a circle to another player in a different circle as the players are jogging around.

Coaching points: The players need to be aware of the position of the receiving player when timing the pass. All players must be ready to receive a pass at any time.

Progression: As confidence increases within the group, so too should the speed of the drill.

drill 20 moving circles

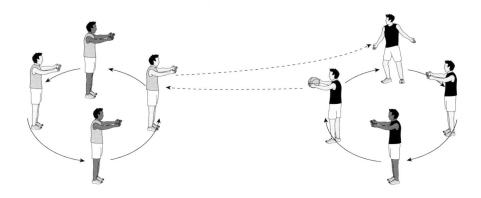

Objective: To practise passing and receiving whilst moving.

Equipment: Eight players and one ball.

Description: Two circles (8 m in diameter and alongside each other) are formed with four players in each circle. The players in one circle jog in a clockwise direction, whilst the players in the other circle jog in an anti-clockwise direction. The ball is passed between players from one circle to the other. The coach can ask the players to change direction and encourage faster or slower movement.

Coaching points: The players need to focus on timing the pass, always being aware of the ball and to provide a target for the ball when receiving.

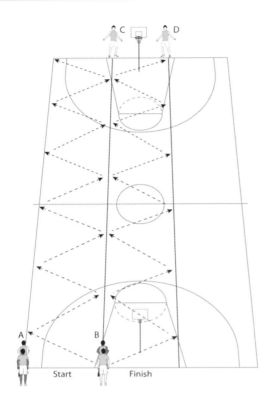

Objective: To improve passing and receiving whilst practising 'step, slide' footwork.

Equipment: Players in pairs with one ball, full court and cones.

Description: Players are divided into pairs with one ball. The players start at positions A and B. The players face each other 5 m apart on the left side of the basket on the base line. The cones are used to divide sections of the court from basket to basket to create the work spaces. The first pair chest pass the ball to each other whilst moving up the court in a 'step, slide' motion. When the first pair reach the halfway line, the next pair follow. Once the players have travelled the length of the court, they join the other lines (C and D) in the next lane and return to the original baseline.

Coaching points: The players should bend their knees and take care not to cross their feet when sliding. Encourage follow-through with arms and hands after making the pass.

drill 22 wall pass

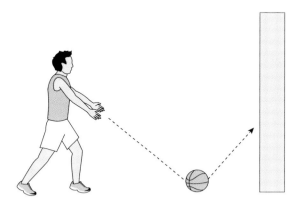

Objective: To practise and improve the bounce pass.

Equipment: One player, one ball and a wall.

Description: The player stands 2 m from the wall and executes a bounce pass against the wall, continually catching and passing.

Coaching points: The player pivots and steps into each pass, and should aim to bounce the ball towards the floor to bounce approximately 1 m from the wall. Players should make a 'snap' motion with the wrists on release of the ball and a follow-through with arms and hands.

Progression: The players can vary the distance for passing according to their ability and the coach can introduce timed races against the clock or races between the players to develop speed.

Objective: To improve passing and receiving skills whilst developing coordination.

Equipment: One player, one ball and a wall.

Description: Each player begins by standing 50 cm away from the wall and makes a chest pass against the wall. The player continues to pass the ball at speed, yet after each pass, takes one step further away from the wall until they are 4 m away. The player then continues to pass, but takes a step forward after each pass. This drill can continue for three minutes.

Coaching points: The players should follow correct passing technique. Emphasise the importance of following through with the arms and hands after each pass and stepping into each pass.

Progression: To increase the speed, the coach can set a target for the number of passes within set time limits.

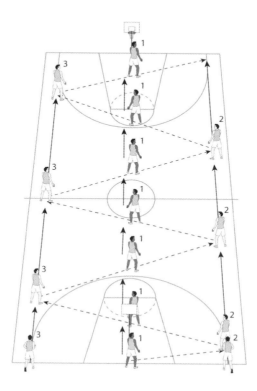

drill 24 'three player' pass and move

Objective: To develop passing skills, and footwork whilst passing and moving.

Equipment: Three players with one ball and half of the court.

Description: The players form three lines on the baseline 4 m apart. The middle player starts with the ball and passes to the player on the right, the ball is returned to the middle player and then passed to the player on the left. The sequence continues whilst the players jog up the court. When the players pass the halfway line the next three begin the same drill. Once a group reach the end line they jog around the outside of the court and back to the starting point before changing roles.

Coaching points: The players should concentrate on correct footwork to avoid travelling when catching and passing; they should also provide a 'target' with their hands for receiving a pass.

Progression: Once confident with passing, a shot at the basket can be added at the end of the drill.

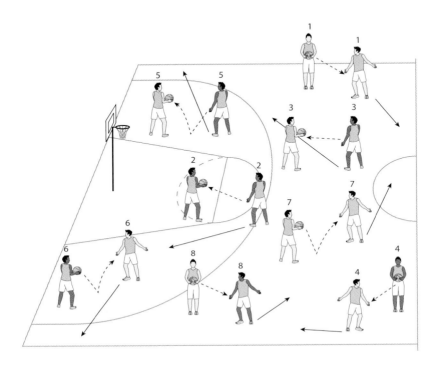

Objective: To encourage players to make decisions whilst passing and moving in a congested area.

Equipment: Pairs with one ball and half of the court (16 to 20 players).

Description: The pairs start approximately 1 m apart within the half court area. They can make a chest pass or a bounce pass to each other. Every time a pass is made by a player, they must then move to another position and signal for the ball from their partner. The passing player must be aware of the other moving pairs within the half court and may choose to delay the pass, select an appropriate pass, pivot before passing or wait for their partner to move to a better receiving position.

Coaching points: The receiving player must be encouraged to use appropriate footwork to get free and receive a well-executed pass. Good clear signals for the ball from the receiving player are crucial.

drill 26   dribble and pass

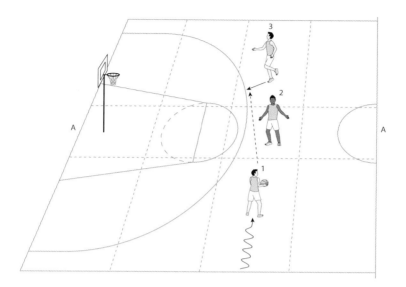

Objective: To improve the chest pass and bounce pass following a dribble.

Equipment: One ball per group of three players.

Description: The court is divided into lanes that are 2 m wide and extend across the width of the court with a 1 m square area marked in the middle of the lane (area A). Player 1 starts with the ball on the sideline. Player 2 is the defender and waits in the middle of the court in area A. Player 3 is positioned at the far end of the court, yet still within the lane. As player 1 begins to dribble towards player 2, player 3 moves behind player 2 and offers a target for a pass from player 1. When player 1 approaches area A, they must attempt to make a pass to player 3, but they cannot use an overhead pass. Player 2 must attempt to intercept the pass. Once a successful pass has been made the players then return to their original positions, but player 3 now starts as the dribbler.

Coaching points: The players should be encouraged to make a firm pass, fake before passing and pivot to create a better position for receiving an appropriate pass. The player receiving the pass should offer a clear target with their hands. The players must remain within the 2 m lane.

Progression: Depending on the ability level of the group, the players can perform set roles for five minutes, or this drill can be performed as a 'piggy in the middle' drill. This would mean that the player who makes a mistake would move to the defensive position. The defender would have to steal the ball in order to move out of the box.

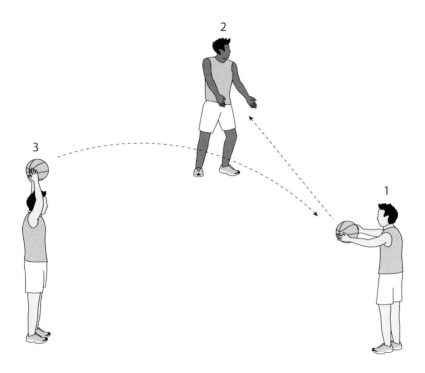

Objective: To improve basic passing technique and to highlight the importance of using different passes.

Equipment: Three players and two balls.

Description: The players form a triangle standing 2 m apart. At the beginning of the drill, player 1 and player 3 hold the basketballs. Player 1 makes a chest pass to player 2, player 2 will then make a bounce pass to player 3. Player 3 will make an overhead pass to player 1. Once player 1 has made the first pass, they should immediately pivot and signal to receive the overhead pass from player 3. The two balls will move quickly and players need to make sure their receiver is empty handed before making a pass. The drill can continue for two minutes and the players can then change roles.

Coaching points: The players should make good, firm passes and follow through with their arms and wrists whilst maintaining correct footwork. At all times the players should signal for the ball before receiving a pass.

Progression: Once confident, the players can increase the speed of the drill and if appropriate can engage in races against other teams.

drill 28 square drill

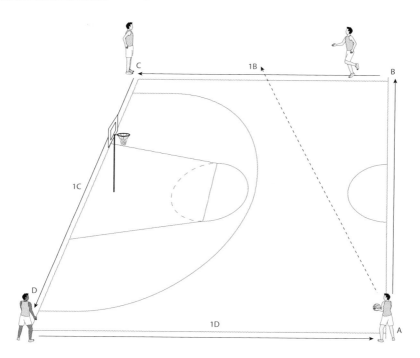

Objective: To improve passing and to encourage players to move after making a pass.

Equipment: Twelve players, two balls and half of the court.

Description: The players form four lines in the corners of the half court in positions A, B, C and D on the diagram. The first player in position A passes to the first player in position B, who should signal with their right hand after taking a step on the halfway line towards position C. The player from B then catches the ball and passes to the first player from C who receives the ball, whilst moving towards position D, again, staying on the side and signalling with the leading right hand. All players who pass must join the back of the line that they pass to. Once the players are confident, the coach can then introduce a second ball at the start of the drill, which would mean that the first players to pass are in positions A and C. Each time the drill breaks down, the balls should go back to positions A and C before re-starting.

Coaching points: The players should signal for the ball with their leading right hand whilst moving towards the next corner of the square. The players should step into the pass and ensure they use correct pivot footwork at all times. They must make good, firm and accurate passes or the drill will break down.

Progression: The coach can introduce targets for the number of passes within a set time which will create some game-type pressure.

Kobe Bryant of the Los Angeles Lakers protects the ball and keeps his head up as he dribbles against Orlando Magic.

DRIBBLING

Dribbling is an important technique for players to master and particularly important in a one on one situation and when setting up an attacking play. There are a range of different techniques that can be developed.

Key principles to remember

- Place the hand on top of the ball with fingers spread

- Always push (not slap) the ball firmly to the floor

- The height of the bounce may vary, but predominantly it should be no higher than waist height and no lower than the knee

- Keep the head up to observe opponents and recognise teammates who may be in a better position

- Use the body to shield the ball from oncoming defenders

- Master the dribbling technique with both hands

Enthusiastic players will spend endless hours practising dribbling on their own and this can be easily done with a ball and hard surface.

drill 29 stationary dribble

Objective: To introduce players to basic dribbling techniques.

Equipment: One player and one ball.

Description: The players begin in a stationary position and dribble the ball with the right hand; the left foot should be forward and knees bent. On the coach's command, the players will change dribbling hands and body position.

Coaching points: The players should keep their head up, relax the body and keep their knees bent. The players should bounce the ball no higher than their waist and no lower than knee height. The ball should be pushed (and not slapped) downwards with the pads of the fingers, whilst coordinating the arm and wrist in motion. The players should also practise using the body to protect the ball from defenders.

Progression: When the players gain confidence and develop a rhythm technique that incorporates the whole body, the speed of the instructions from the coach can also be increased.

drill 30 dribble on the move

Objective: To improve dribbling speed and control, whilst moving and changing direction.

Equipment: One player with a ball each and the full court.

Description: The players begin in a stationary dribbling position. The coach calls out the number 'one' and the players begin to move around the court whilst dribbling in different directions. The coach calls out number 'two' and the players get down on one knee and continue to dribble; the coach calls out the number 'three' and the players move into a sitting position on the floor, whilst still dribbling the ball; the coach calls out the number 'four' and the players lie on their backs and continue to dribble the ball. The coach may also call 'change' at any time which indicates a change of hands. The numbers do not have to be called in numerical order.

Coaching points: The players must maintain sound technique with the ball to the side of the body, using the body to protect the ball from a potential defender. The players need to be aware of others dribbling in different directions and therefore need to look up to avoid any potential collisions. Players are encouraged to continue to dribble without catching the ball at any time, which will reinforce 'double-dribble' and 'travelling' rules.

Progression: The coach can change instructions and call the numbers more quickly to test the reactions and the ball control of the players.

drill 31 zig-zag dribble

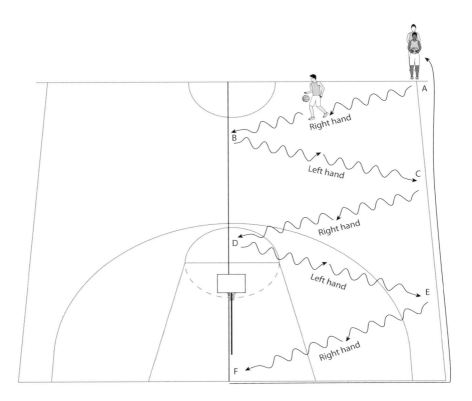

Objective: To develop confidence and control when changing hands and direction whilst dribbling around the court.

Equipment: A quarter of the court, four to six players with a ball each and cones.

Description: The players are divided into groups in a quarter of the court. Six cones are evenly distributed in a zig-zag formation. The players line up at position A and dribble with the right hand towards position B; when one step away from the cone, the players change the dribbling hand and direction and head towards position C. The same pattern continues until finishing at position F when the player will then loop around the cone and return to the start point at position A.

Coaching points: The players should be encouraged to keep their head up, and maintain correct body and ball position to ensure the protection of the ball from potential defenders.

Progression: Once the players are confident, a defender can be introduced and players can switch roles.

Objective: To practise protecting the ball against a defender whilst dribbling.

Equipment: Ten to twenty players, one ball each and half of the court.

Description: All of the players, with the exception of two defenders, dribble around the half court with a ball each. The coach shouts 'go' and the two defenders (crocodiles) attempt to steal the ball from the dribbling players. Once a crocodile has successfully and fairly stolen a ball the player who has lost the ball will become a crocodile and must attempt to regain a ball. The crocodiles must not foul. The players with the ball must give it up if they lose possession, travel or double-dribble (when a player dribbles the ball with two hands simultaneously or stops dribbling and then dribbles again). The coach should call 'stop' at three minute intervals to monitor the success of individual players and to change the crocodiles.

Coaching points: The player dribbling the ball should be encouraged to keep their head up and protect the ball with their body and utilise a range of techniques.

Progression: The coach can use more crocodiles as the group improves. The players can record the number of times that they become crocodiles in each practice.

drill 33 dribbling at speed

Objective: To dribble the ball at speed whilst developing control with either hand.

Equipment: Groups of six players, one ball and two cones.

Description: Two lines of players face each other, 8 m apart. The first player in line A dribbles the ball in a straight line and when 1 m away from the opposite line executes a jump stop and hands the ball to the first player waiting and then joins the back of line B. The player in line B who has received the ball, then dribbles towards line A and performs the same action. A jump stop involves a player catching a ball whilst moving or dribbling and landing on one or two feet.

Coaching points: Whilst increasing the speed of the dribble, the players are still encouraged to dribble with the correct technique and keep their head up.

Progression: The coach can encourage confident players to practise with either hand or bring in advanced dribbling skills (cross-over, through legs, behind back etc.).

Objective: To practise dribbling, whilst changing pace and improving court awareness.

Equipment: Twelve to sixteen players, four balls and four cones.

Description: The cones are placed to form a cross formation 6 m apart. The players are evenly distributed and stand behind the four cones; the players at the front of each line have a ball each. Upon the instruction of the coach, the first player in each line dribbles the ball to the opposite line (line A travels to line C, and line B travels to line D) and the player 'jump stops' before handing the ball to the waiting player and joining the back of the opposite line. When the players reach the middle of the cross, they must make a decision in order to avoid a collision with the other three approaching players (stop and observe whilst using a stationary dribble, cross-over dribble, slow down, go faster etc.). The players cannot stop the dribbling action until they reach the opposite side.

Coaching points: The players should keep their head up and be aware of the movements of the other players at all times.

Progression: The coach can guide the group in terms of the speed of the drill or make the cross smaller to increase pressure on the players when crossing over.

drill 35 crossroads and slide

Objective: To practise dribbling whilst changing pace, and improving court awareness.

Equipment: Twelve to sixteen players, four balls and four cones.

Description: The cones are placed to form a cross formation 6 m apart. The players are evenly distributed and stand behind the four cones in a line; the players at the front of each line have a ball each. On the instruction of the coach, the first player in each line dribbles the ball to the opposite line (line A travels to line C, and line B travels to line D) and jump stops before handing the ball to the waiting player and joining the back of the opposite line. When the players reach the middle of the cross they must make a decision in order to avoid a collision with the other three approaching players (stop and observe whilst using a stationary dribble, cross-over dribble, slow down, go faster etc.). The players cannot stop the dribbling action until they reach the opposite side. Once the dribbling player has released the ball to the player waiting at the front of the opposite line, they proceed to the back of the opposite line and facing outwards, they use the defensive 'step, slide' motion to join the back of the line to their right. Consequently, A will finish at D, B will finish at A, C will finish at B and D will finish at C.

Coaching points: The players should keep their head up and be aware of the movements of other players when dribbling. The players adopting 'step, slide' movement should keep their knees bent and maintain correct posture when moving to the different lines.

Progression: The coach can guide the group in terms of the speed of the drill or make the cross smaller to increase the pressure on the players when crossing over.

drill 36 traffic lights

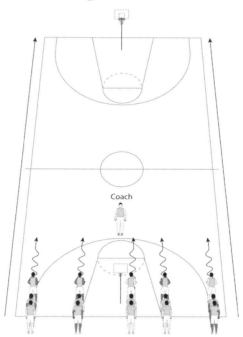

Coach

Objective: To improve dribbling technique, whilst encouraging players to keep their head up.

Equipment: Six to twenty-four players with a ball each and the full court.

Description: The players stand along the baseline in groups of four to six, facing the coach who is 5 m away. The coach makes the following signals with his hands which prompt specific dribbling actions from players. The players follow the guidelines one group at a time. (1) Thumb up: dribble forwards; (2) Thumb down: dribble backwards; (3) Open palms: stationary dribbling; (4) Outstretched right hand: dribble left; (5) Outstretched left hand: dribble right. The coach walks backwards as he makes the signals and the players move towards him as they dribble. When the dribbling group have reached the free throw line at the opposite end of the court they then dribble around the outside of the court and rejoin the waiting players at the start point. All waiting players should be encouraged to practise stationary dribbling skills whilst they wait for their turn to follow the signals and move up the court. The coach moves back to the original starting point to signal to the next group.

Coaching points: The players must keep their heads up at all times to follow the signals of the coach and to avoid collisions with other players.

Progression: The coach can introduce a range of competitions as players aim to make the minimal amount of mistakes whilst performing the drill as an individual or within a team.

drill 37 shadows

Objective: To improve dribbling technique whilst changing pace and direction.

Equipment: Pairs with one ball and a full court.

Description: The players are divided into pairs. One player starts with the ball and takes the role of the leader, whilst the partner takes the role of the shadow. When the drill begins the leader must dribble the ball around the court and attempt to lose the following shadow who is attempting to stay within 1 m of the leader at all times. The players will change roles after two minutes.

Coaching points: The leader must keep their head up and be prepared to attempt to change hands, pace and direction. More advanced players can execute more complex skills.

Progression: This drill can also be used with the focus on defensive footwork for the 'shadow' player.

Objective: To develop skills in dribbling at full speed against a chasing defender.

Equipment: One ball per pair, cones and the full court.

Description: The players form two lines behind the cones in position A at the free throw line and position B on the baseline. The players in position A are the dribblers and their partners in position B are the chasers. The coach will give a signal to begin and the player in position B will pass the ball to the player in position A who will dribble the full length of the court to the far basket and attempt a lay-up shot. The trailing player in position B must chase the attacker after making the pass and attempt to block the shot. The players then return around the outside of the court to positions A and B, but change roles. Whilst players are returning to their starting positions, another pair can begin the same drill.

Coaching points: It must be emphasised that the aim should be for the attacking player to move quickly and reach the target with the least amount of bounces of the ball as possible.

Progression: The coach can modify the starting points of the players to accommodate the different ability levels.

drill 39 forty second weak hand drill

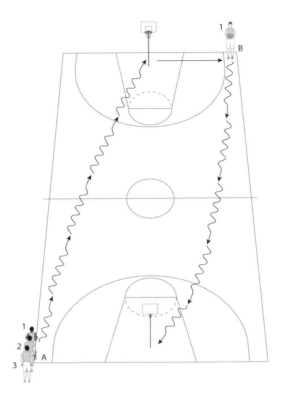

Objective: To improve technique and speed with the weaker hand whilst dribbling and performing a lay-up shot.

Equipment: One player with one ball and the full court.

Description: Right-handed players begin the drill from position A and dribble up the court with their left hand and attempt a left-handed lay-up. The player then rebounds the ball after the shot and performs the same skill in the opposite direction from point B. The player continues with this sequence for forty seconds and attempts to make six lay-ups. Left-handed players would use their right hand on the opposite side of the court.

Coaching points: The players should use their weaker hand, keep their head up and bounce the ball slightly ahead with a forceful pushing motion of the hand.

Progression: The coach can introduce team relay challenges or individual scoring competitions that can be timed.

drill 40 dribble and steal

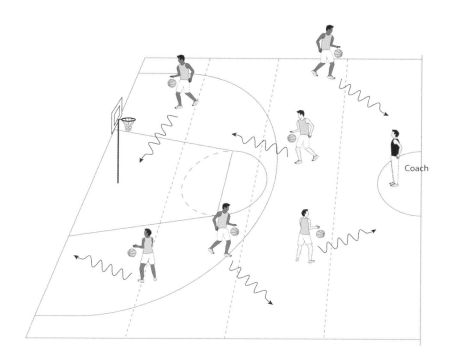

Objective: To develop listening and awareness skills whilst dribbling the ball.

Equipment: Twelve to twenty-four players with one ball each and half of the court.

Description: All players begin by continually dribbling the ball in different directions, using different skills and techniques in the half court. On the coach's command all players must place their own ball on the floor and then quickly collect a different ball that has been released by another player and then continue with the dribble. The coach will identify the last player to retrieve a ball, who will then leave the half court area. The players who are eliminated will spend the short period in between games practising stationary dribbling as they observe the active members in the drill.

Coaching points: Players should be encouraged to keep their head up to avoid collisions with other players and to be aware of rolling balls. When the balls have been placed on the floor, the players should maintain a low body position and use defensive footwork as they look for another ball.

drill 41   grab the prize

Objective: To develop ball handling, and awareness when dribbling.

Equipment: A ball for each player (10 to 16 players), bibs or tag belts, and half of the court.

Description: Each player has a ball and wears a tag belt or tucks a bib into their shorts. The bibs or belts are the prizes that all of the players are chasing. Once the game starts, players must dribble the ball continually whilst moving around the half court. The task for the players is to attempt to steal a prize from other dribbling players. Once a prize has been secured, the successful player can hand it to the coach and go in search of more prizes. The players who lose a prize can dribble the full length of the court and then return to the game in search of regaining a prize (they can ask the coach for a replacement, if they have previously secured one from another player). This drill continues for five minutes and the coach can then see who has secured the most prizes and who is actually still wearing a belt or a bib.

Coaching points: The players should protect the ball when dribbling at all times and keep their heads up. A range of dribbling skills will be needed to escape defenders (change of pace, crossover dribble, behind back dribble, roll etc.).

drill 42 dribble relays

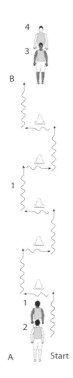

Objective: To develop pace and control whilst dribbling the ball.

Equipment: Balls and cones.

Description: Divide the players into teams of four. Place five cones in a straight line, one metre apart from point A to point B. Two players stand at either end of the line and 1 m away. On the coach's command, the first player at position A dribbles to the right of the first cone with the right hand; once around the cone, the player changes to the left hand and this sequence continues until the ball is passed to the first player who is waiting 1 m away from point B. The player at point B makes a return journey from B to A and follows the same dribbling sequence. This continues until all players have completed one journey.

Coaching points: The players should bounce the ball slightly ahead at approximately waist height.

Progression: More experienced players can perform a behind the back dribble when changing hands at the cones.

Objective: To improve control when handling and dribbling.

Equipment: One ball per player and a wall.

Description: The player stands half a metre away from the wall and dribbles the ball against the wall at head height. The player will make 20 contacts with their favourite hand and then change and use the other hand. This drill can continue for five minutes. The players may also work in pairs and alternate the observer and the dribbler role.

Coaching points: The players should use the pads of their fingers when contacting the ball with a 'pushing' motion rather than a 'slapping' motion.

SHOOTING

Shooting is probably the most popular fundamental skill for players of all ages and levels. Whilst many players develop specialist areas of the court that they can score from, it is vital that young players learn to shoot from all areas of the court, both near to and far from the basket, regardless of their body height. Some coaches tend to commit younger players to specific positions at an early age (e.g. taller players only practise skills associated with the forward player's role), however this should be avoided.

Key principles of set shooting

▨ Start in triple threat position (both hands holding the ball)

▨ Feet should be shoulder-width apart and knees bent, yet straight on release

▨ Move the ball to head height and hold the ball in one hand with the arm in an 'L' shaped position (non shooting hand protects the ball)

▨ One hand releases the ball with the fingers of the shooting hand spread and placed behind the ball

▨ The elbow bends into the body and then the shooting arm moves forward, before following through with arm, wrists and fingers in the direction of the basket.

Lay-up shot

Within the game of basketball, when an attacking player observes a gap in the opposition's defence they may wish to execute a lay-up shot which enables the player to score closer to the basket and consequently increases the rate of scoring success. All players should learn to shoot both right- and left-handed lay-ups.

Key principles to the lay-up shot

▨ When dribbling towards the basket at speed, protect the ball

▨ Use correct footwork (right-handed lay-up: step right and then left)

▨ After taking the second step, take the ball towards the basket with two hands and gain as much height as possible

▨ Whilst in the air, place the right hand behind the ball and with outstretched arms, push the ball off the top corner of the small square near the basket.

Linas Kleiza of Lithuania demonstrates excellent technique and concentration when executing this shot.

drill 44 sit and shoot

Objective: To develop a fundamental shooting action with an emphasis on improving the upper body position.

Equipment: One chair and one ball.

Description: One player sits on a chair holding a ball and a partner stands 1 m away with arms outstretched facing the chair. The sitting player then shoots the ball 20 times into the outstretched arms of the partner. The partner records how many times the ball lands in his hands directly. The players then change roles.

Coaching points: The players should hold the ball in the palm of their shooting hand, elbow under the ball forming an 'L' shape with their arm. The players should push the ball and follow through with their arms and hands towards the basket as if waving goodbye.

Progression: Once the players are confident and have developed sound techniques, the basket can be introduced as a target.

drill 45 wall shooting

Objective: To develop shooting action and rhythm without the pressure of scoring the basket.

Equipment: One player, one ball and a wall.

Description: The player stands 2 m away from the wall, tosses the ball in the air and catches the ball whilst facing the wall. The player then pivots into the correct footwork position for a set shot and shoots the ball against the wall towards a visual target, approximately three metres high. Repeat this sequence for 3 minutes.

Coaching points: The player should have their shooting hand behind the ball, bringing the ball between their shoulder and ear with their elbow underneath the ball. The player's feet should be shoulder-width apart and the knees should be bent. On the release of the ball, the player should extend their legs and elbow and follow through with arms and hands.

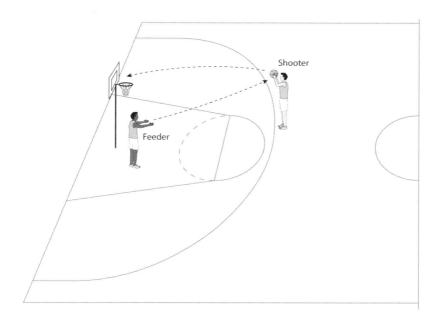

Objective: To practise shooting after receiving a pass, whilst using correct footwork and sound shooting technique.

Equipment: One ball per pair and a basket.

Description: One player is given the role of shooter and the partner is given the role of rebounder and feeder of the ball. The shooter starts outside the zone and receives a pass from the feeder. Once the shooter has successfully made a basket, they move into another position outside the zone and signal to receive another pass. The shooter takes 20 shots and then the players change roles.

Coaching points: The shooter should signal for the ball before receiving the pass. When receiving the pass, the shooter should pivot if necessary to ensure a balanced shooting position which will encourage sound technique.

Progression: Advanced players can use an additional ball which encourages the players to shoot at speed. The distance from the basket can also be increased.

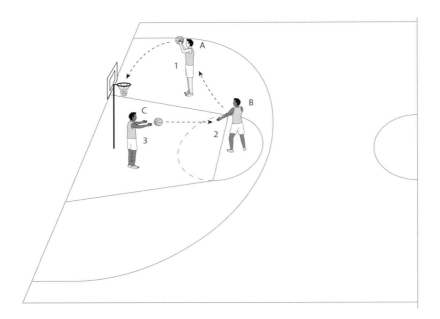

Objective: To improve shooting at game speed.

Equipment: Three players, two balls and one basket.

Description: One player stands in a shooting position (A) outside the zone, the second player stands in position B as a feeder on the free throw line and the third player stands in position C as the rebounder. The rebounder and feeder start with the balls. The feeder (B) passes to the shooter (A) who shoots the ball. The rebounder (C) passes the ball to the feeder and then rebounds the first shot. The feeder continues to pass to the shooter (A). This sequence continues so that the shooter is continually shooting for two minutes. The players then change roles.

Coaching points: All of the players should perform all of the tasks and be reminded about sound fundamentals for shooting, passing and rebounding.

Progression: Once the players become confident in performing the drill, scoring targets can be set for each player that relate to their ability level.

Objective: To improve shooting when faced with a defender.

Equipment: Two players, one ball and a basket.

Description: The shooter (B) takes up a position outside the zone. The defender (A) stands underneath the basket with the ball and passes to the shooter who signals for the pass. The defender follows the pass and extends their hands to place basic pressure on the shooter. The shooter takes the shot and then follows the shot, collecting the rebound whilst the defender has switched to the role of shooter. The sequence continues for five minutes.

Coaching points: The shooters need to position their feet quickly and look for an early release of shot whilst maintaining the correct technique.

Progression: The players can transfer the drill to different areas around the basket and as the confidence of the shooter grows, the defender can increase the pressure.

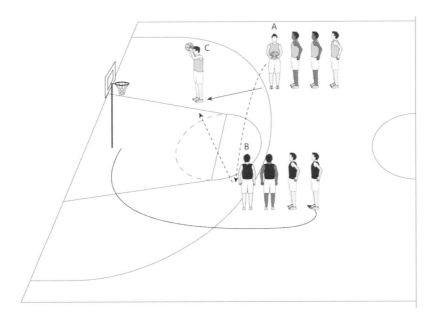

Objective: To improve shooting skills, following passing and movement around the court.

Equipment: The players are divided into pairs with one ball and a basket.

Description: The players face each other 2 m apart at the top of the zone in positions A and B. The other members of the team join the lines with one ball between each pair. The player on the right (A) starts with the ball and makes a bounce pass to their partner (B) and then moves 2 m towards the basket (position C) whilst still remaining outside the zone. The ball is then returned to the player in position C who shoots the ball. Player B then rebounds the shot and both players join opposite lines and change roles.

Coaching points: Whilst executing the skills of passing, shooting, receiving and rebounding, the correct footwork and technique for the skills should be re-enforced. The shooting player must signal for the ball with the right hand as they move towards the basket.

Progression: The same drill can be used to practise shooting from nearer to the basket, the other side of the basket or further away from the basket.

drill 50 knockout

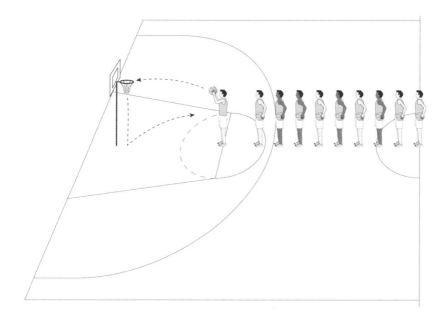

Objective: To improve free throw shooting whilst encouraging players to rebound their own missed shots. This is an excellent team activity at the end of the practice.

Equipment: Ten players with a ball each and one basket.

Description: The players form a line facing the basket from the free throw line. The first player (1) in the line shoots the ball and if successful, collects the rebound and joins the back of the line. Should the player miss the shot, they must attempt to score from the rebound as quickly as possible before the next player (2) in the line scores from the free throw line and knocks them out of the game. Once a basket has been scored by player 1 or 2, player 3 then joins the game and the sequence continues. The player remaining at the end of the game is the winner.

Coaching points: The players should focus on developing a good free throw routine with sound technique and concentration, yet be ready to follow the shot to make a good rebound.

drill 51 make and move

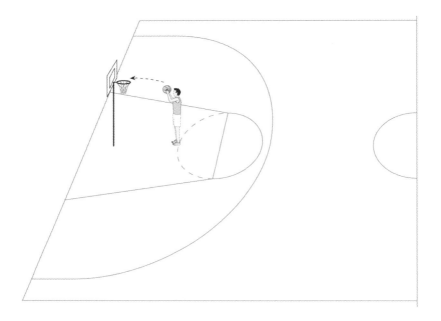

Objective: To practise shooting at various distances from the basket.

Equipment: One player, one ball and a basket.

Description: The player begins one step away from the basket and shoots the ball. If successful they then take one step back and shoot again. If unsuccessful the player must take a step forward. The drill should last for ten minutes and several other players can use the same basket for the drill, but from different starting points.

Coaching points: The players should concentrate on maintaining sound familiar shooting techniques whilst thinking about the distance from the basket when judging the force of the throwing action.

Progression: The coach can introduce pressure by setting scoring targets within a set time.

drill 52 twenty-ones

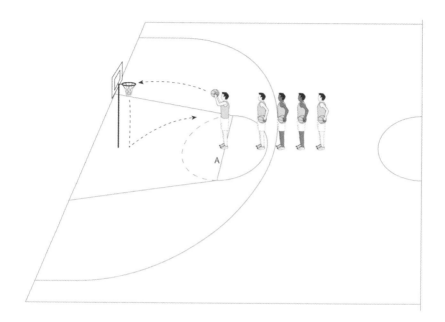

Objective: To practise the free throw whilst encouraging players to follow the shot and rebound the ball.

Equipment: Five players with a ball each and one basket.

Description: The players are placed in a shooting group and stand in a line positioned on the free throw line at position A. The first person in the line holds the ball and shoots from the designated area and is awarded two points for a successful shot. Should the player score or miss, they are allowed to follow the shot and take a rebound shot for one point, yet the ball must not bounce more than once before the second shot is made. The player then goes to the back of the line. The first player to reach 21 points wins, yet all players can concentrate on their own progress with their own score.

Coaching points: Players need to focus on good shooting technique and also be prepared to act quickly to rebound.

Progression: The coach can introduce a rule that rewards players who score with the first shot and the rebound, to return to the free throw line immediately and only go to the back of the line if they miss one of the two attempts. The drill can also be used at various positions around the zone.

drill 53 team lay-up drill

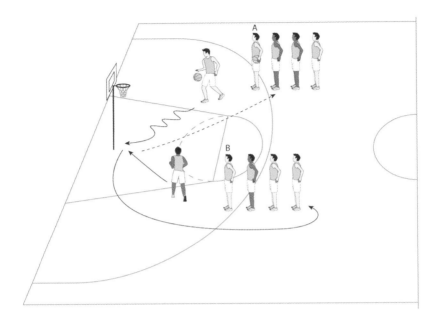

Objective: To practise the lay-up shot, passing and rebounding as a team.

Equipment: Ten players, two balls and a basket.

Description: The players form two lines, 2 m away from the zone at positions A and B. The first two players in line A start with a ball. The first player dribbles towards the basket and performs a lay-up shot (leaving the ball) and immediately joins the back of line B. The first player in line B moves towards the basket, collects the rebound and passes to the third player in line A and then joins the back of line A. Whilst this is happening, the second player in line A who has a ball is dribbling to the basket to attempt a lay-up shot. This sequence continues.

Coaching points: Players performing lay-up shots are encouraged to drive strongly to the basket and release the ball with an outstretched arm and close to the basket, whilst pushing the ball against the corner of the small square on the backboard to help with accuracy. The rebounders are encouraged to take the ball at the highest point with outstretched arms and then release the pass quickly after executing correct pivot footwork.

Progression: The players can keep an individual score, or the team shooting into one basket can compete against the team using another basket. The coach could also set a target of successful baskets within a set time.

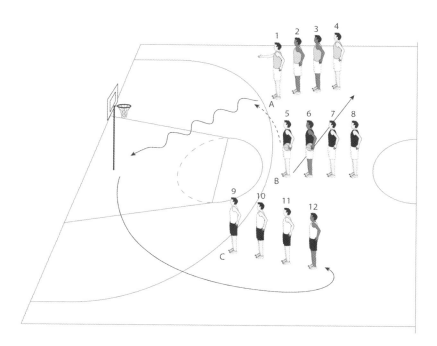

drill 54   outlet drill

Objective: To practise the lay-up shot, rebounding and the outlet pass.

Equipment: Twelve players, two balls and a basket.

Description: The players are divided into three lines of four players at positions A, B and C. The first two players in line B hold a ball each. To begin the drill, the first player in line B makes a pass to the first player in line A who should be moving towards the basket. The passing player (B) then joins the back of line A. The player who has received the pass performs a right-handed lay-up and joins the back of line C. The first player in line C rebounds the lay-up shot and passes to the player in line B and then joins the back of line B. In the first instance, once the player from line A has made a shot, the second ball from line B is passed to the second person in line A. This sequence then continues.

Coaching points: The players receiving the ball must give clear signals with their hands as a target for the pass. Rebounding players must time their actions and once they have caught the ball, should pivot whilst protecting the ball before making an outlet pass to line B.

Progression: In this drill the ball can also be passed to the left side for all players to practise left-handed lay-ups. Players can keep an individual score or the team shooting into one basket can compete against a team using another basket. The coach could also set a target of successful baskets within a set time.

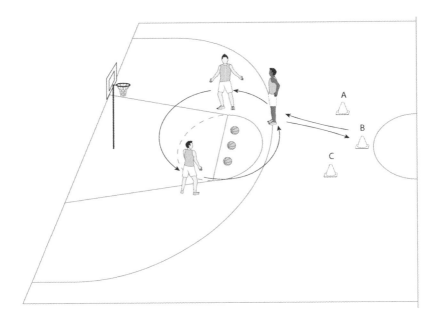

Objective: To practise shooting under pressure and develop footwork and movement around the court.

Equipment: Three players, three balls and cones.

Description: The balls are placed inside the circle at the top of the zone and the three players, on the signal of the coach move around the circle in defensive 'step, slide' motion, facing the balls. On the coach's command, the players must sprint to touch one of the markers in positions A, B and C that are placed in a triangle, 1 m away from the three point line. The players then return, running to collect a ball and shoot until they score. Balls are then placed in the circle and the drill begins again.

Coaching points: The players should use the correct defensive footwork when sliding feet and keep their head up to be aware of the movements of the other players.

Progression: The players can decide on the most appropriate shot to take (set shot, lay-up) or the coach could set targets to improve specific skills.

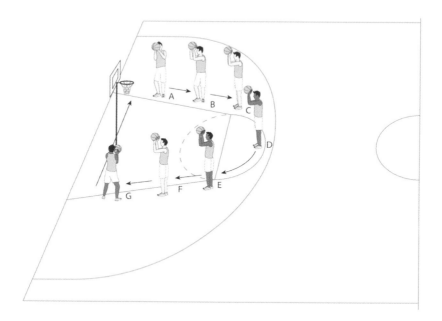

Objective: To improve shooting from different areas near to the basket.

Equipment: Seven players per basket with one ball each and cones.

Description: Seven shooting points (A to G) are identified around the zone. The players can start at any point, yet must move from letter to letter in the correct sequence. Once a player has scored from a set position, they can then move to the next letter. If the player misses a shot, they must continue to shoot from that point until they score. The players must count how many attempts it takes to move around the seven areas.

Coaching points: Despite being surrounded by other players shooting the ball, the players must time their own shot to avoid balls clashing and also concentrate on performing balanced shooting technique. This creates a game-like situation as players often have to shoot immediately or delay the shot.

Progression: The players can keep a record of their scores and use the drill throughout the season to monitor their progress.

drill 57 trail, shoot and break

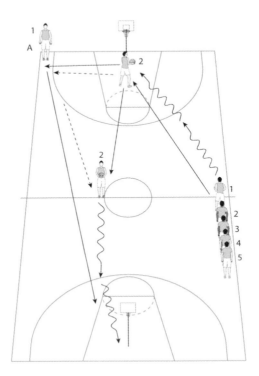

Objective: To practise lay-up shots, rebounding and fast break plays.

Equipment: Pairs with one ball and the full court.

Description: The players are divided into pairs and form a line from the halfway line facing the basket at the side of the court. Player 1 dribbles towards the basket, performs a lay-up shot and then cuts to the corner of the court (A). The trailing player (player 2) follows the shooter, takes the rebound before the ball reaches the floor and then passes to the shooter who has moved to point A. Following the pass, player 2 then runs towards the basket at the far end of the court and signals for the ball with a leading left hand as they approach the halfway line. Player 1 then uses a javelin pass to feed player 2 who then dribbles and performs a lay-up shot. Player 1 follows the pass and takes the rebound and the drill continues. The speed of the drill and ability level will depend on how many pairs can operate. When using the drill with advanced players, the number of players that can take part can be increased.

Coaching points: The players who are breaking to the basket must receive the ball with an outstretched arm rather than reaching back to collect the pass. The passing players must follow through with arms and hands after releasing the ball and always be aware of the target.

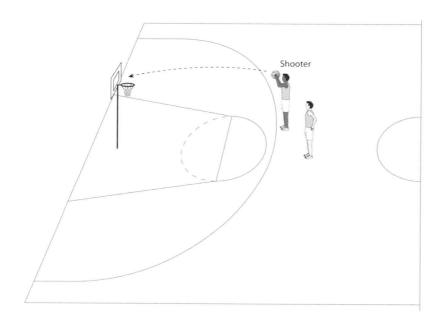

Objective: To practise shooting from different areas of the court.

Equipment: Pairs with one ball and a basket.

Description: The first player selects a position and shoots from that position on the court. If the player scores, their partner takes a shot from the same position. If player 2 also scores then player 1 selects another position and shoots. If player 2 misses the shot then they receive an 'R' for rookie (the players can remember who has been awarded an 'R'). If player 1 misses and player 2 scores, then player 1 receives a letter and player 2 selects the next starting position. Once 'rookie' has been recorded by a player the game is over.

Coaching points: The players should select shots that they are confident of making or they can use the drill to practise shooting from their weaker areas, but should always relate to areas that they shoot from in a real game situation.

drill 59   spinning wheel

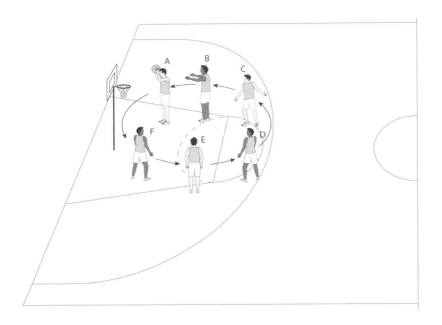

Objective: To practise shooting after receiving a pass.

Equipment: Six players, one ball and a basket.

Description: The players stand in positions A to F to form a circle around the zone. They keep moving around the circle in an anti-clockwise direction after a shot has been taken at position A. The player who shoots passes to the next player arriving at point A and moves to position F. This is a fun activity that allows players to both perform and observe.

Progression: The drill can be used to increase competition between individuals, or the players can record the number of missed and scored baskets.

drill 60 speed shooting

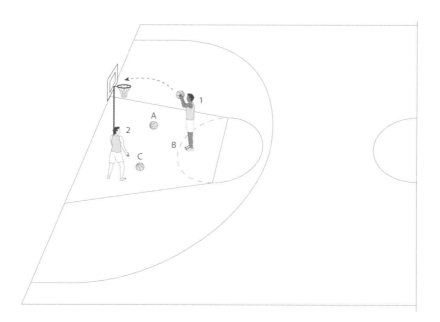

Objective: To improve shooting at speed within the zone and to develop fitness.

Equipment: Two players, three balls and one basket.

Description: The balls are positioned in a triangle 1 m apart and near the basket in positions A, B and C. Player 1 stands ready to shoot and player 2 will rebound the balls and place them back in position. On the coach's command, player 1 must attempt to score as many baskets as possible at close range in a one minute period. Following each shot by player 1, player 2 places the ball back on its spot whilst player 1 shoots the next ball, following the sequence A, B, C.

Coaching points: When collecting the ball, the players should bend their knees and 'explode' with their shooting action to release the ball as near to the basket as possible with outstretched arms. The players should also use the pivot technique to maintain the correct shooting position.

Progression: The coach can introduce competitive races between team members or encourage the players to keep a record of their personal best scores.

drill 61 shooting roundabout

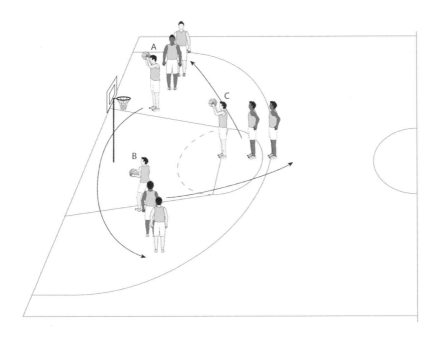

Objective: To improve shooting after receiving a pass.

Equipment: Nine to twelve players, three balls, one basket and cones.

Description: The players form three lines, 1 m from the zone in a triangular formation (A, B and C). The first player from each line shoots the ball, collects their own rebound and then passes the ball to the player at the front of the next line. The player from line A rebounds and passes to the awaiting player in line B, B to C and C to A. The players then join the back of the line that they have passed to.

Coaching points: Players awaiting a pass must signal for the ball and use the correct footwork to ensure a good shooting stance (pivoting if necessary).

Progression: Players can be set individual or team targets for scoring against a team using the other basket, or this can be a timed drill.

shooting over a static defender after a dribble

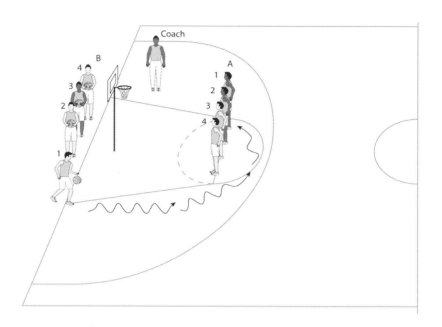

Objective: To introduce beginners to shooting over an opponent.

Equipment: Eight players, four balls and a basket.

Description: Four defenders are numbered 1 to 4 and stand at the top of the zone with their back to the basket (line A). Four attackers are numbered 1 to 4 and stand along the baseline with a ball each (line B). The coach shouts a number from 1 to 4 and the named attacker dribbles towards and around line A, then picks out and shoots over the top of his opposite number who is a static defender. The defender collects the rebound and goes to the baseline (line B) and the shooter replaces the defender in line A.

Coaching points: When approaching the defender the attacker should use a jump shot, look at the basket and use the correct pivot footwork to gain a balanced shooting position.

Progression: Once confident, players can dribble at speed and shoot over more active defenders. The coach can allocate attackers against different numbered defenders to improve the concentration of the players.

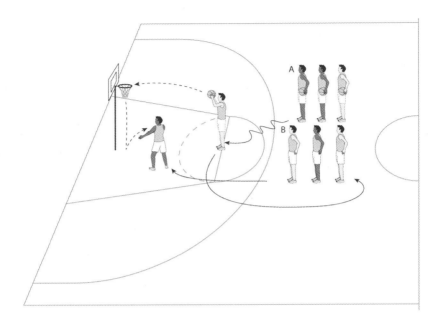

Objective: To introduce beginners to shooting after taking an offensive rebound.

Equipment: Eight players, four balls and a basket.

Description: The players form two lines, 2 m apart with four players in each line, 2 m from the three point line (A and B). The players in line A begin with a ball each. The first player from line A dribbles the ball to the free throw line and shoots at the basket with the intention of missing. The first player in line B follows the shooter and the ball, attempting to collect the rebound from the missed shot and shoots from close range. The players then jog around the sideline to join the back of the opposite line.

Coaching points: The rebounding players must take the ball at the highest point with outstretched arms. Once the rebounder lands, they should bend their knees and jump straight back up and shoot with outstretched arms and direct the ball off the backboard.

Progression: Once the players become more advanced, the drill can be done at speed so all the waiting players have to be aware at all times. At a later stage, the first shooter in the drill can also contest the rebound after the missed shot.

REBOUNDING

Rebounding is the responsibility of all the players in a team, yet too often there is an assumption that the taller players should win all of the rebounds. Many shots in a game of basketball are missed shots, consequently, a team that can rebound the ball successfully will create more second shots offensively. At the defensive end of the court, good rebounding technique will limit scoring opportunities for opponents and for teams winning defensive rebounds, the likelihood of creating a fast break offence will increase. The key to good rebounding depends on the player gaining a good blocking out position in the first instance.

Key principles

▨ When a shot is taken, watch the ball and the oncoming opponent

▨ Using the pivot motion and facing the basket, block the path of the opponent, with feet spread wide apart, knees bent and arms outwards

▨ From the blocking out position, continue to watch the ball and the opponent

▨ Jump aggressively off two feet and reach towards the ball, to grab it with two hands and outstretched arms.

Once the ball has been claimed:

▨ Defensive – pivot away from the basket and pass to a teammate

▨ Offensive – bend knees and go back up towards the basket with outstretched arms, and push the ball off the backboard.

Carl Landry of the Sacramento Kings shows the importance of boxing out and gaining a good position, before taking a rebound against Antawn Jamison of the Cleveland Cavaliers.

Objective: To improve rebounding in a competitive situation.

Equipment: Four players, one ball and a basket.

Description: The players find a space inside the zone and face the basket. The players A1 and A2 work together and the players B1 and B2 work together. The coach stands outside the zone at various positions and feeds the ball against the ring or the backboard. The players work in pairs to block out the opposing pair and then take the rebound before the ball touches the floor. A point is awarded for each successful rebound and the groups rotate when the first pair reach five points. Observing teammates can then replace the players that have been active. It is a physically demanding drill and rest periods are necessary before beginning the next phase.

Coaching points: The players must be aware of the ball and the other players rebounding, so that they can get in a good position to block out at an early stage. The players should be encouraged to take the ball at the highest point possible.

Progression: The coach can integrate this drill into a three versus three mini-game, with a clear emphasis on rebounding.

drill 65 partner box out

Objective: To develop the determination and improve the technique required to box out an opponent.

Equipment: Two players, one ball and four cones.

Description: The two players stand inside an area 3 m x 2 m, marked with four cones. The ball is placed on the end line. The players take turns in taking a defensive rebound position with the aim of protecting the ball from their partner. The other player is challenged to legally fight past the defender to touch the ball. The challenge should last for thirty seconds, but the coach can utilise several areas for a large group and change partners within the group.

Coaching points: The defensive player should spread their feet wider than shoulder-width apart, bend their knees and extend their arms to box out. The feet should be placed firmly on the floor, however 'step, slide' footwork can also be used to block the path of the partner.

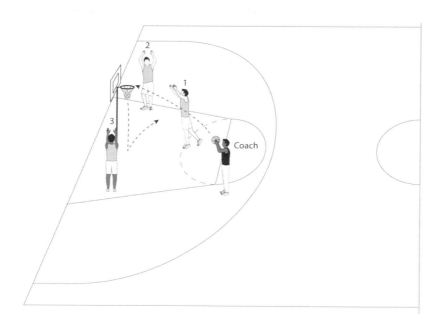

Objective: To improve rebounding and shooting in a competitive situation.

Equipment: Three players, one ball and a basket.

Description: The players are numbered 1 to 3 and form a triangle around the basket with a 1 m distance between each of them. The coach shoots the ball to miss the basket and the three players compete for the rebound. The player winning the rebound should then attempt to go straight back up towards the basket with the ball, with the intention of scoring. If the rebounder misses, the three players try to rebound the ball again. Upon the completion of a basket, the ball is returned to the coach. The three players go back to their starting positions and the coach repeats the exercise. Once a player has scored three baskets, the active players then rest and the coach can bring in three more players. The coach can determine how many groups of players are included in the rotation, yet the players should repeat the drill at least three times. This is a physically demanding drill.

Coaching points: When the shot goes up, the rebounding players should keep an eye on the flight of the ball and attempt to get in a good position to block out the other players. Following the rebound, if the shooters are under pressure they should be encouraged to fake before shooting.

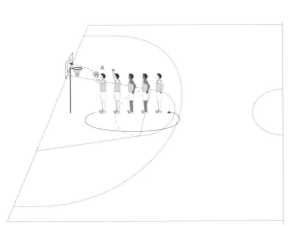

Objective: To improve timing, balance, agility and jumping when rebounding.

Equipment: Five players, one ball and a basket.

Description: The five players form a line, 1 m from the front of the backboard (A). Player 1 throws the ball gently against the backboard and returns to the back of the line. Player 2 then jumps off two feet, catches the ball in the air with two hands and pushes the ball back against the backboard before landing. Player 2 then runs to the back of the line. The players in the line then follow this sequence. The drill can continue for 20 tips and can conclude with a basket being scored.

Coaching points: The rebounder should jump off two feet to ensure control of the body, extend the arms and catch with two hands at the highest possible point. The players should land on two feet, shoulder-width apart and bend their knees. They should be encouraged to use correct pivot footwork when turning after 'the tip'.

Progression: The coach can use this drill with more than one backboard and introduce races between different groups.

drill 68 balloon battle

Objective: To improve timing, endurance and positioning when developing rebound skills.

Equipment: Two players, centre or shooting circle and one balloon.

Description: Two players stand inside the circle. A balloon is fed above the players' heads and the players have to jump continually and compete for the most touches of the balloon by pushing it into the air whilst attempting to stay within the circle. Players can box out and move for the best position, but must not break any body contact rules. The drill lasts for forty-five seconds.

Coaching points: The players must think about the position of their partner and the position of the balloon when 'boxing out' and timing the jump.

Progression: The coach can increase the area and the number of people within the teams.

drill 69 block out circle

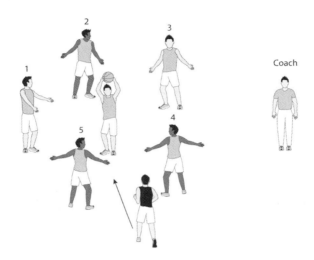

Objective: To introduce beginners to the principles of 'blocking out' before rebounding the ball.

Equipment: Six players and one ball.

Description: The players numbered 1 to 5 are positioned in a circle, arm's length apart. The player in the middle is the defender (6) and stands with the ball high in the air with outstretched arms. The coach calls out the number of a player in the circle and that player must move outside the circle and attempt to touch the ball and move past the players who are blocking out. The attacking player must not foul the other players forming the circle who are protecting the ball and the defender. When the ball has been touched or after ten seconds, the attacker must return to their position in the circle. The coach then calls another number and the task is repeated. The coach changes the player in the middle after three minutes.

Coaching points: The blocking players must bend their knees, have their feet spread apart and use outstretched arms to protect the ball.

Progression: The players can also jog whilst in the circle, before a number is called and then block out. This can be related to moving in a game situation.

Objective: To improve rebounding and then pivoting away from the basket whilst developing conditioning and coordination.

Equipment: One player, one ball and a wall.

Description: The player faces the wall and stands half a metre away, whilst holding a ball. The player tips the ball against the wall five times with the right hand. The player then jumps and catches the ball with outstretched arms in two hands and lands on both feet at the same time. They complete a 180 degree turn by pivoting on the right foot and back to the starting position. The player then completes the same action, but tips with the left hand and pivots on the left foot. They should continue for one minute before resting and then repeating the drill.

Coaching points: The player should rebound the ball at the highest possible point, place the pivot foot firmly on the floor and protect the ball with both hands whilst turning.

drill 71 offensive rebounding

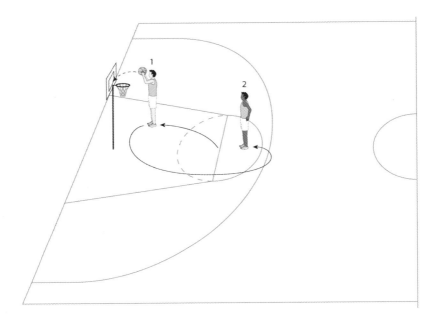

Objective: To improve offensive rebounding.

Equipment: Pairs, one ball and a basket.

Description: Player 1 starts on the free throw line and then, moving towards the right side of the basket, feeds the ball off the backboard. The player then jumps towards the ball with arms outstretched and grabs it with two hands at the highest possible point. The player then lands on two feet and points elbows outwards whilst protecting the ball at chest height. Player 2 then follows the same actions whilst player 1 loops around the back of the zone and returns to the starting point. Once the coach is satisfied with the basic rebounding technique, the players then add an explosive jump back up to the basket after collecting the rebound, followed by a shot off the backboard.

Coaching points: The rebounder should jump off two feet to ensure control of the body, extend the arms and catch with two hands at the highest possible point. The players should land on two feet, shoulder-width apart and bend their knees. When driving back towards the basket, the player should bend the knees, protect the ball and then extend the arms when exploding towards the basket.

Progression: The role of player 2 can change to that of a defender when trailing player 1, to create a more realistic situation. The players can complete 10 attempts before changing tasks.

DEFENCE

The two main forms of defensive play are man-to-man defence and zone defence. When working with young players, the coach should emphasise the importance of playing man-to-man defence and help the players to develop the key principles. Whilst zone defence can be effective, many youngsters struggle to develop the correct footwork and enthusiasm when engaging with the more stationary approach of covering a zone. It is also my belief that if youngsters develop good man-to-man fundamentals in their formative years, they are more likely to perform effectively in zone defence later.

Developing fundamental individual defence skills can be very challenging for the coach and particularly young players as they often place greater importance on receiving acclaim for scoring. It must be noted however, that attitude and determination carry just as much importance as ability; consequently, once players become more experienced and defend effectively in more structured games, the value and appreciation of good defensive play will increase.

Principles for on ball defence

- Within the defensive stance, the player should have feet slightly wider than shoulder-width apart and bent knees, staying on the balls of their feet

- The defensive player should be an arm's length away from an opponent who has not used the dribble. Once the offensive player has dribbled and stopped, the defender should close in and stop a pass, shot or try to steal the ball

- Keep the body lower than the opponent, yet keep hands up and palms facing the opponent

- Use 'step, slide' motion when following the opponent and do not cross the feet

- Always be aware of the ball and other events on the court – quick feet and hands are crucial.

The importance of hard work, correct footwork and good use of hands when playing defence is highlighted by Luol Deng of Chicago Bulls and Great Britain.

drill 72   sit and catch

Objective: To become familiar with the defensive stance position and to improve reactions and hand speed.

Equipment: Two tennis balls per pair.

Description: Player 1 takes up a body position as if sitting on a chair with feet shoulder-width apart. Player 2 takes the position facing player 1, half a metre away holding one ball with outstretched arms at shoulder height. Player 2 drops the ball and player 1 has to catch the ball with one hand. Once player 1 has achieved this, player 2 holds a ball in each hand and alternates the ball releasing from each hand to increase pressure on player 1. The coach will instruct players to change roles after three minutes.

Coaching points: The player who is receiving the ball should have the palms of their hands facing upwards.

Progression: Once the players gain confidence, the task can become more competitive with the player who is dropping the ball 'faking' before release in an attempt to catch the receiver out. The tennis balls can also be replaced with coins.

drill 73 dynamic defence

Objective: To develop speed, improve defensive footwork and develop court awareness, whilst reacting to the attacking player.

Equipment: Players, one ball and half of the court.

Description: The coach stands on the halfway line holding one basketball and faces the group who find a space each throughout half of the court. The coach bounces the ball once and catches it. The group must react quickly and move into a defensive body position stance and shout 'ready'. The coach then places the ball in his outstretched right hand and the group slide in that direction (their left). The coach then alternates hands and the group must watch and change direction accordingly. At any time, the coach can place the ball in both hands and slap the ball; at this stage the watching group must stutter their feet on the spot. All of the actions prepare the defender for movements they may use when faced with an attacking player in a game.

Coaching points: The players must maintain a low body position when moving their feet at all times.

Progression: The coach can introduce an additional range of visual directions from the stutter position to create game-like movements for the players.

Developments: The coach can create a range of additional movements that can encourage the players to respond to game situations.

Objective: To improve fitness, teamwork and defensive footwork.

Equipment: Six players and one third of the court.

Description: Four players form a circle and they all touch hands, but do not link. One further player (1) remains within the circle and is nominated as the target and should be protected by the players in the circle. Another further player (2) stands outside the circle and is given the task of tagging the target player (1) within thirty seconds. The circle must move to block the tag. The players rotate roles until everyone has played in each position.

Coaching points: The players within the circle must use footwork and 'step, slide' motion with their feet, keeping the body low and maintaining a defensive stance position.

Progression: Once the players become more advanced, the coach can allow player 1 within the circle to attempt to escape and reach player 2.

Objective: To improve agility, speed, coordination and defensive footwork.

Equipment: Half of the court and cones.

Description: The players stand in a defensive stance position between two cones placed 3 m apart. The players move from side to side using correct defensive 'step, slide' motion. They must touch the marker with the leading hand on every journey. The aim is to count the number of times a marker is touched.

Coaching points: The players should be encouraged to maintain the correct defensive position and keep their heads and hands up and stay low throughout the drill. It is crucial that players do not cross their feet.

Progression: This drill can be used as an individual or team relay race.

drill 76 mirror step drill

A

B

Objective: To improve defensive footwork and reaction speed when faced with an offensive player.

Equipment: Pairs with one ball and cones.

Description: Two cones (A and B) are placed 3 m apart and players face each other between the cones with each player either side of the imaginary line. The offensive player begins with the ball and whilst facing his opponent and maintaining eye contact, dribbles from cone to cone. Neither player should cross the imaginary line. Once the offensive player gains confidence with the drill, they can then attempt to move at a faster speed with the ball, vary the direction and change the dribbling hand. The offensive player must remain within the coned area. The defender must use correct defensive 'step, slide' motion to attempt to mirror the offensive player at all times. If at any time the defender loses the offensive player, they must recover their mirror position and try again to hold and maintain eye contact. The drill can last for three minutes, then the players can change roles.

Coaching points: The players should be encouraged to maintain the correct defensive position and keep their heads and hands up and stay low throughout the drill. It is crucial that players do not cross their feet.

Progression: When working with more advanced players, the coach can call out instructions to the offensive player to encourage forward and backward movements that will encourage the defender to develop other aspects of footwork.

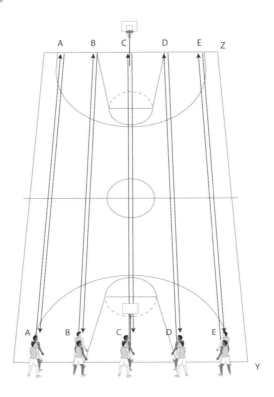

Objective: To improve conditioning and defensive footwork.

Equipment: Ten players, full court and cones.

Description: Five cones are placed along the baseline, 2 m apart in positions A, B, C, D, E (line Y). Further cones (A, B, C, D, E) are placed on the baseline (line Z) at the far baseline at the other end of the court. The players line up behind a cone at line Y and following instruction from the coach, move at speed using the defensive 'step, slide' motion towards the opposite cone. Once they touch the cone with their leading hand, they turn and make the return to the original cone, whilst still using appropriate footwork. The players lead with the right foot on the first trip and the left foot on the return trip. The awaiting five players then step into position whilst the first five players recover, before the next trip.

Coaching points: The players should be encouraged to maintain the correct defensive position and keep their heads and hands up and stay low throughout the drill. It is crucial that players do not cross their feet.

Progression: The coach can use this drill over a short period and use a limited number of repetitions with the aim of improving footwork. Increasing the number of repetitions can develop fitness.

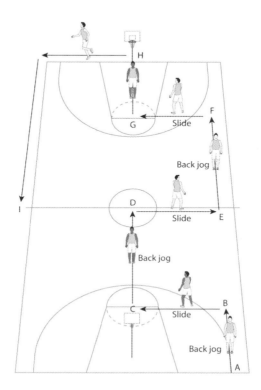

Objective: To warm up the body and improve defensive footwork.

Equipment: Cones and the full court.

Description: The players form a line at the right hand corner of the court on the baseline. The first player at point A, jogs backwards to point B and then takes up a defensive stance body position and leading with the left foot, step-slides to point C; the player then jogs backwards from C to D; step-slides from D to E (leading with the right foot); jogs backwards from E to F; step-slides from F to G (leading with the left foot) and jogs backwards from G to H. The players then sprint from H to I. On the coach's command the other players will start at various intervals. The players then walk back to the starting position.

Coaching points: The players should be encouraged to maintain the correct defensive position and keep their heads and hands up, but stay low with the body throughout the drill when using the 'step, slide' motion. It is crucial that players do not cross their feet.

Progression: The coach can introduce time targets related to completions of the circuit.

GAME SCENARIOS

The drills in this chapter can be used to introduce younger players to game situations, and they can also be used by more experienced players to practise specific scenarios that they too will face in competitive games. Most of the drills will give the players the opportunity to improve both offensive and defensive play and it is crucial that they do not waste any practice time by neglecting a skill. The more realistic the practice becomes, the greater the chance that players will improve.

Many young players who participate in a range of games often practise and learn skills and techniques in an isolated situation. The coach should always attempt to relate all practices to the challenges that players will face in game situations, both in terms of skills that will be needed and decisions that will have to be made. The players need to learn to think for themselves and think strategically in a game situation, so this should be considered in planning the sessions.

The players should be encouraged to perform all of the skills and play in all of the positions. It is vital that young players do not focus upon one type of role when they practise and the coach must aim to develop players with a multi-dimensional approach which will ensure greater development at a later stage.

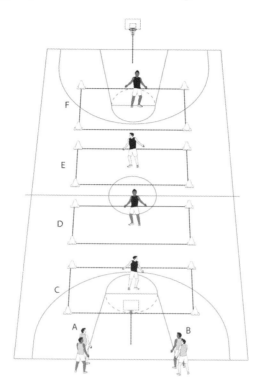

Objective: To improve passing in small areas of the court when faced by a defender.

Equipment: Eight to twelve players, cones and one ball for each pair.

Description: Two players stand with a ball underneath the basket, 3 m apart on the baseline in positions A and B. The cones are then placed to form 4 m x 4 m square grids through the centre of the court (C, D, E and F). A defender is positioned in each grid and must remain within that area throughout the drill. The two attacking players then have to move through each grid and successfully pass to each other whilst using 'step, slide' footwork and staying 3 m apart. If the attacking players lose control, they must go back and join the other pairs in the group who are waiting to attack. The coach alternates defenders after a set time.

Coaching points: Whilst being aware of the positions of the defenders, attacking players should fake before the pass and vary the types of pass.

Progression: Once the players successfully reach point E, scoring a basket can be introduced.

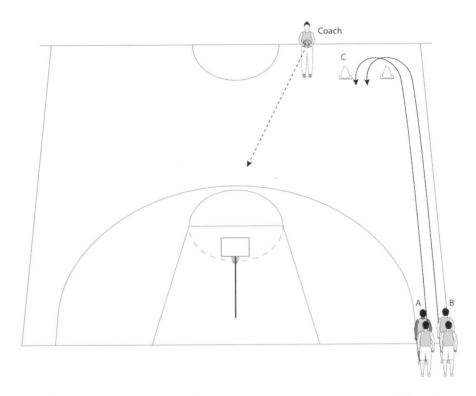

drill 80 hustle and attack

Objective: To encourage players to compete for a loose ball and then improve attacking and defending in a one against one situation.

Equipment: One ball, half of the court and cones.

Description: The players form two lines in the corner of the court on the baseline in positions A and B. Two cones are placed 1 m from the halfway line on the court and 1 m from the sideline in position C. The coach stands beside the two cones and on the coach's command the first two players in the line jog together towards C. Once the players have looped around the cones at C, the coach releases the ball towards the basket situated on the baseline. The first player to collect the ball becomes the attacker and the other player becomes the defender.

Coaching points: The defender should recover quickly from losing the ball and move to block the path to the basket for the attacking player. The attacking player, on gaining the ball should look at the position of the defender and consider the appropriate individual attacking options (drive to basket, shoot, or fake and drive to basket).

drill 81 cross court – one versus one

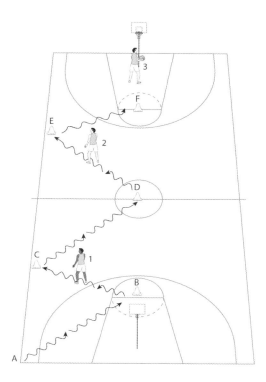

Objective: To improve control of the ball and increase the variety of dribbling techniques that can be used against a defender.

Equipment: One ball per attacking player, three defenders, the full court and cones.

Description: Assemble the players at point A in the corner of the court on the baseline. Cones are then placed in a zig-zag pattern at 5 m intervals (B, C, D, E, F) over the length of the court. The defenders are placed at positions B, D and F. The first player dribbles the ball from point A, and once reaching point B, the designated defender has to try and steal the ball (in a passive way in the early stages) as the attacker attempts to reach point C. Once the player successfully reaches point C, they continue to dribble unopposed to point D where a defender is waiting. Once again, the attacking player has to get past the defender to reach position E. If successful again, the player then dribbles to point F and has to beat the final defender, before attempting to score.

Coaching points: The offensive player must keep their head up, use either hand, protect the ball and be prepared to change pace and type of dribble (e.g. crossover, behind back, roll etc.).

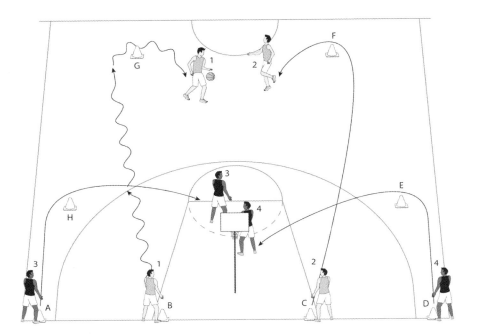

Objective: To improve attacking and defensive skills and encourage players to make decisions.

Equipment: One ball per group of four players, half of the court and cones.

Description: The players line up at four points, 3 m apart on the baseline and facing the court. The defending players (3 and 4) stand at positions A and D and the attacking players stand at positions B and C. On the coach's command, player 1 dribbles the ball to point G, whilst player 2 runs to point F. Once they have looped around the cones they attack the basket. Meanwhile, defenders 3 and 4 have looped around positions E and H and have taken up a defensive position. The players will then contest a two versus two game situation. Once a basket has been scored or control is lost by the attacking team, the players change roles and join the different lines on the baseline.

Coaching points: The players should be encouraged to create space for each other and pass quickly if there are no attacking opportunities open. At all times, both sets of players should use correct offensive and defensive footwork.

Progression: When working with more advanced players, the coach can set the defenders the target of only becoming attackers in the drill that follows once they have stopped the basket from being scored in the existing drill. Consequently, a successful attacking team will remain as attackers in the next sequence of play.

overload offence

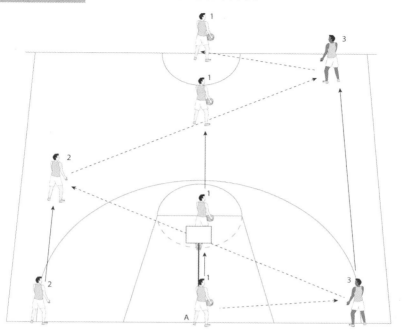

Objective: To encourage players to think, select and perform appropriate skills when attacking the basket and facing a defender.

Equipment: Three players, one ball and half of the court.

Description: The three players begin by standing along the baseline. Two of the players (2 and 3) stand near each of the sidelines and the other player (1) stands under the basket at position A, facing the halfway line. Player 1 starts with the ball and makes alternate passes to the players 2 and 3 who each return the ball to player 1 after receiving each pass. The three players move towards the halfway line as they pass and receive the ball. Whichever player has possession of the ball, once the players reach the halfway line, must place the ball on the floor and sprint back towards the basket (A) and become the defender. The diagram shows that player 1 is the defender on this occasion. The remaining two players (2 and 3) will then attack the basket against the defender. Once a basket has been scored or the defender regains possession, the drill is over and the players rejoin the baseline where other players will be waiting to repeat the drill. This drill can be used at both ends of the court at the same time.

Coaching points: The attacking players, when in possession of the ball, must show an awareness of the defender's position. The attacking players should recognise when a teammate is free and should then make a pass, or if their teammate is marked by the defender, there should be a space for them to go to the basket themselves. The attackers who are not in possession should also be thinking of creating space for their teammate with appropriate movements away from the ball.

Objective: To encourage players to think, select and perform appropriate skills when facing defenders.

Equipment: Five players, one ball and the full court.

Description: The three attacking players begin by standing along the baseline marked A. Two of the players (2 and 3) stand near each of the sidelines and the other player (1) stands under the basket and facing the halfway line. The central player (1) starts with the ball and makes alternate passes to the players 2 and 3 who each return the ball to player 1 after each pass. The three players move towards the halfway line as they pass and receive the ball. The other two players (4 and 5) have taken up defensive positions at the front and back of the zone in area B, but must not advance past the dotted line (C) which is 2 m from the zone they are defending. Once the three attackers cross the halfway line, the defenders become more of a threat and the attacking players then have to make decisions related to passing, dribbling and shooting. Once a basket has been scored or if the defenders spoil the attack, the two defenders become the attackers towards basket A and player 1 who started in the middle of the three players becomes the defender. Once an attack ends, the departing players that are no longer involved in the drill join the line of players under the nearest basket formed by other members of the group who are waiting to participate.

Coaching points: When in possession of the ball the attacking players must be aware of the defenders' positions when making decisions and moving off the ball.

drill 85 drive to basket

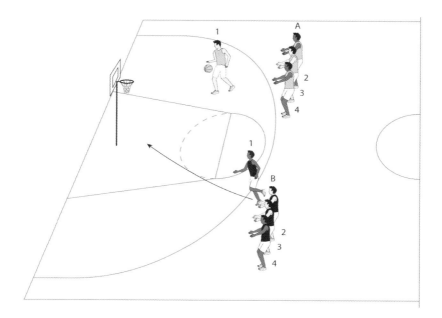

Objective: To encourage players to perform lay-up shots against defenders.

Equipment: Pairs, one ball and half the court.

Description: The players form two lines, A and B, that are positioned either side of the court and outside the three point line facing the basket. In both lines the players are given a number 1 to 4. The players in line A hold the balls and are the attackers. The players all stand in a ready position and the coach calls a random number between 1 and 4. The awaiting players must react and the player in line A will attack the basket and the player in line B with the same number should quickly take up the position of the defender. Once the attack has finished, the players rejoin the opposite line and ensure that they change roles.

Coaching points: The attacking player must be aware of the position of the defender and then drive directly to the basket, fake and drive to the basket, or shoot at an early stage.

Progression: The coach may decide to place an additional attacking player at the top of the zone to encourage attacking players to utilise teammates during an attack.

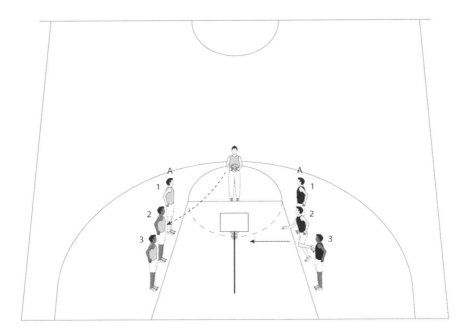

Objective: To encourage players to make decisions and perform offensive skills near the basket.

Equipment: Six players, one ball and half of the court.

Description: Three players are positioned on each side of the zone in positions A and B. The players are numbered A1 to A3 on side A and B1 to B3 on side B. The coach is positioned at the top of the zone, holding the ball. When the coach passes the ball to one of the players, the opposite number must defend, e.g. if A2 receives the pass, B2 is automatically the defender. The players have to think and act at game-speed, and react and make decisions as attackers or as defenders. Once the offence is complete, the ball is given back to the coach and players return to their places and await the next pass from the coach. The coach will change the positions of the players after a set time.

Coaching points: The attacking players must react quickly and respond to the position of the defender and be ready to fake after receiving a pass. The defenders must also react quickly and move to block the main path to the basket for the attacker, whilst moving towards the shooter to limit shooting opportunities.

Progression: The coach can vary the positions of the players around the zone after a five minute period.

Objective: To encourage the players to make decisions and perform offensive skills near the basket in a one versus one situation.

Equipment: Pairs, one ball and a basket.

Description: The players are positioned in two lines: line A is positioned on the baseline by the side of the zone and line B is positioned at the top corner of the zone facing the basket. The first player in line A is the defensive player and rolls the ball towards the first player in line B who is the offensive player. The player from line B, on receiving the ball has to decide which offensive action to take as the defensive player from line A moves towards them.

Coaching points: When attacking players receive the ball they should face the basket in a triple threat position and consider the options to shoot, drive to the basket, or fake and drive to the basket.

Progression: The coach can assign different attackers to different defenders to create a more realistic game-like situation.

drill 88 half court, non stop – two versus one

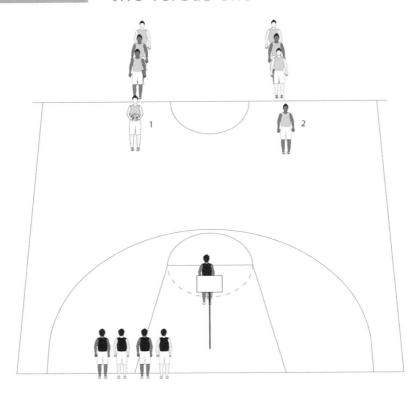

Objective: To introduce teamwork and decision making when playing against a defender.

Equipment: Three players, one ball and half of the court.

Description: The two offensive players start with the ball on the halfway line and the one defender takes a position within the defensive zone. When a basket is scored by the attacking team, they are rewarded with one point. Should the defender prevent the basket from being scored, they are rewarded with two points. The players then go to the back of the waiting line for attackers and defenders, whilst the next group of players begin. This drill can involve a large number of players and roles can be changed at the discretion of the coach. The reward of points will ensure that the defenders are motivated throughout the drill.

Coaching points: The attacking players, when in possession of the ball, must show an awareness of the defender's position. They should recognise when a teammate is free and should then make a pass, or if their teammate is marked by the defender, there should be a space for them to go to the basket themselves. The attackers who are not in possession should also be thinking of creating space for their teammate with appropriate movements away from the ball.

drill 89 shoot on sight

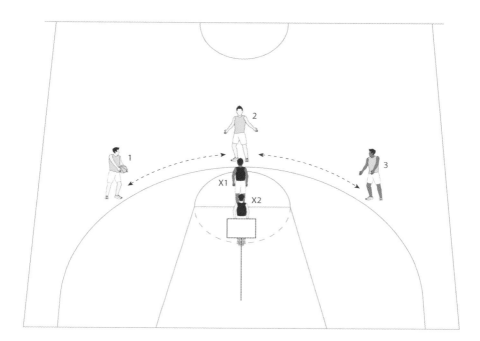

Objective: To encourage players to shoot when open and free from defenders.

Equipment: Five players at a time, one ball and half of the court.

Description: Two defenders are placed within the zone and numbered X1 and X2. The three attacking players are placed around the three point line at least 2 m apart. The attacking players pass the ball to each other until someone is open to shoot, but they should stay within 1 m of their starting position. The defensive players should be encouraged to work hard to intercept the passes and attempt to block the threat of shots. Missed shots can be contested and both sets of players can compete for the rebounds. The attacking team have 10 attempts to build an offence, after which the roles are changed.

Coaching points: The coach should encourage the attacking players to move into a triple threat position when they receive the ball.

Progression: This is also a good practice to improve defensive technique and rebounding and the coach can also place the emphasis on defensive play, thus setting targets for the defensive players.

drill 90   take the lay-up

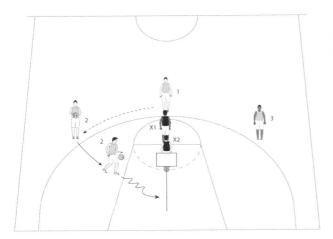

Objective: To encourage beginners to perform the lay-up shot when free from defenders.

Equipment: Five players at one time, one ball and the attacking third of the court.

Description: This is an attacking drill and teams can only score by performing a lay-up shot. The attacking team of three players (1, 2 and 3) start with the ball on the edge of the three point line. The defenders (X1 and X2) begin the drill in a position inside the zone. The attacking team pass the ball to each other until an opportunity exists for a player to take a lay-up shot. Once an attempt at a lay-up shot has been made or when possession is lost, a new attack begins. The team have 10 offensive attempts and the roles then change.

Coaching points: Players must ensure that they keep their spacing when attacking in order to create space and 'stretch' the defence, and to create space to execute the lay-up shot. The passing must be accurate and fast.

Progression: Once the defenders drop towards the basket to counter the lay-up attempt, the attacking players are then permitted to take a set shot. The coach will have to use their discretion when guiding the players in this situation.

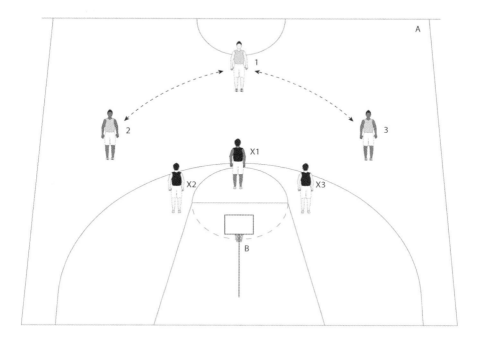

drill 91   three versus three conditioned game

Objective: To gain an understanding of the rules of the half court 'three versus three' mini-game.

Equipment: Six players, one ball and half of the court.

Description: The game begins with three players nominated as offensive players (1, 2 and 3) attacking the basket (B) and three players nominated as defensive players (X1, X2 and X3). The offensive team start with the ball behind the halfway line (A) and the defensive team are positioned within the three point line area. The younger players should be encouraged to play man-to-man defence with a clear aim to develop footwork skills. The standard rules of basketball apply, with the main focus being upon fouls, violations (travel, double dribble etc.) and sideline balls. Once the defending team gains possession of the ball, they must pass or dribble the ball past line A before becoming the offensive team and attacking the same basket (B). The offensive team then become the defensive players and change positions. If the defending team concede a basket, they must pass the ball in from the baseline and clear line A before attacking the same basket.

Coaching points: This drill can be used to develop most types of techniques and strategies in a mini-game situation for both offensive and defensive situations.

Progression: The coach can allow the defenders free access to line A if they are beginners.

Objective: To encourage attacking players to pass and then cut to basket.

Equipment: Six players, one ball and half of the court.

Description: The offensive team are positioned in a triangle, outside the three point line and facing the basket (players 1, 2 and 3). Player 1 begins with the ball and may opt to pass to player 2. Once the pass has been made, player 1 then moves (cuts) towards the basket. Player 2 can then either pass to player 1 or give the ball to player 3 who has now moved into the space that has been left by player 1 at the top of the zone. If player 1 does receive the return pass from player 2, then a shot can be made at the basket. However, if player 1 does not receive the pass, player 2 can alternatively pass the ball to player 3 (now at the top of the zone) and player 1 will continue to move through the zone and into the space that has been left by player 3. The offensive team now have the original starting formation and can run the play again. This is also called 'balancing the floor'.

Coaching points: At all times, the wing players must be moving and using correct footwork to find space to receive a pass. The cutting player must cut towards the basket and not away from the passing player.

Progression: Once the players gain confidence, the coach can allow them to look at their other attacking options and use the space that has been created by the cutting player. Cutting players should look to change pace and direction when approached by defenders.

drill 93   one versus one – deny

Objective: To develop movement from offensive players when attempting to get free for a pass from a teammate.

Equipment: Three players, one ball and a basket.

Description: The three players are each given a role and a starting position. Player 1 is the passer, player 2 is the attacker and player 3 is the defender. The drill begins when player 1 starts with the ball and faces the basket in a ready position, 1 m away from the top of the 3 point arc. Player 2 must attempt to get free from player 3 to receive a pass from player 1, but must not move more than 1 m away from the zone. Player 3 must attempt to deny the pass from player 1 to player 2 by playing aggressive ball denial. Player 2 must move to get open to receive the pass. Once a pass has been made, a one versus one situation is played until a basket has been scored or until possession is lost by the attacking player.

Coaching points: Whilst the offensive player attempts to get free from the marker, the defensive player must take the correct body position and watch the ball and the offensive player. The offensive player must use correct footwork and be prepared to change pace and direction, whilst using body fakes to get free. Once free, the offensive player should use a clear signal with their hands to create a target for the passing player.

Progression: This drill can be developed by introducing two more players to create a two versus two game situation.

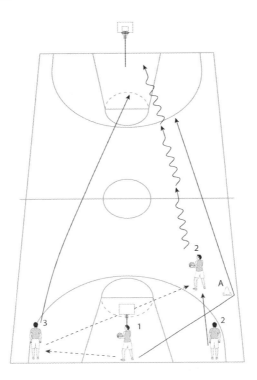

Objective: To improve speed and decision making when attacking the basket against a defender.

Equipment: Three players, one ball, the full court and cones.

Description: One player (1) stands underneath the basket and two players (2 and 3) stand either side of the player on the baseline at a distance of 4 m. On the coach's command, player 1 passes the ball to player 3 who then passes to player 2 who receives the ball at position A, near the three point line. Player 2 then attacks the far basket and player 3 chases as the defender. Once player 1 has made the initial pass, they run and go around the cone at position A and then trail the other two players to act as an additional attacker and teammate for player 2. At both ends of the court, observing players can be waiting behind the baseline to take part. The players who have finished the drill join the lines behind the baseline nearest to their basket.

Coaching points: The attacking player must keep their head up and be aware of the defender's position, yet in the first instance should be encouraged to drive to the basket at speed. However, if the defender manages to block their path to the basket, the attacking player must use the additional teammate (player 1) and look at other attacking options.

drill 95 shell drill

Objective: To introduce the basic principles of man-to-man team defence.

Equipment: Eight players, one ball and half of the court.

Description: The players are divided into two teams of four players each in one half of the court in the positions identified in the diagram. The attacking players are stationary and will pass the ball to each other, around the perimeter of the zone. When the attacking players receive the ball they pivot into the triple threat position. The defending players do not attempt to intercept the ball, but should think about their position in relation to the ball, the player that they are marking and their teammates. If the defender's opponent has the ball, the defender should be applying pressure (player X1 in the illustration). If the ball is one pass away from the defender's player, then they should be denying a potential pass (player X2). If the ball is two passes away from the defender's player then the defender should be in a 'helping' position (player X3). If the ball is three passes away from the defender's player, they should be in a covering position (player X4). Throughout the drill, the coach will blow the whistle to signal a pass. Following the pass, the players pause and the coach can check if the defender has moved to the correct position before blowing the whistle again for the next pass.

Coaching points: The players should keep their heads up to see the ball, other players and the court. The defensive players should maintain correct posture and a defensive stance throughout the drill.

Progression: The drill can become more competitive and realistic once players have shown that they understand the principles.

drill 96 fisherman drill

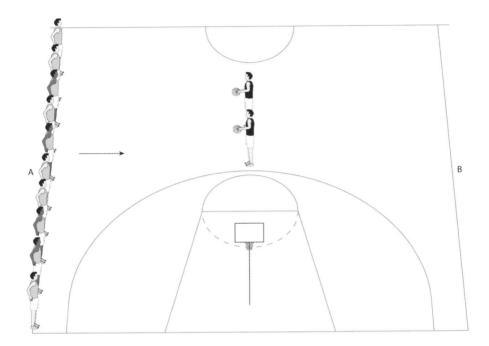

Objective: To improve offensive and defensive footwork and court awareness.

Equipment: Half the court, groups of 10 to 15, two balls and two bibs.

Description: The drill begins with the group standing on the sideline (A). The task for the group is to reach the opposite side of the court (B), but they must await the coach's command before starting. Two defensive players wear a bib and hold a ball each in both hands and stand in the middle of the half-court. The task for the defenders is to touch the oncoming players whilst holding the ball. The two defensive players must stand in a defensive stance position and use defensive 'step, slide' footwork when following or intercepting oncoming players. The players who are touched, leave the court and take up a stationary defensive stance position whilst observing the remainder of the drill. The players who reach the opposite side without being touched must wait for the coach to signal before attempting a return journey. Once all players have been touched, the coach can change the defenders. The coach may use a greater number of defenders if the task proves too difficult for younger children. There must also be an emphasis on safety and the coach may opt to use foam balls and advise the defenders to touch the attackers below the head and above the waist.

Coaching points: The defenders must communicate and work as a team to trap attacking players.

WARMING DOWN

The warm down can be used in many ways, however, the coach should ensure that it meets the needs of the young players in three areas. First of all, it should bring the mind and body back to their pre-activity states and relax the body to avoid stiffness. Secondly, the warm down could incorporate some specific skill aspect that the coach may wish to reinforce (e.g. dribbling, shooting etc.) in a more relaxed way. Thirdly, the coach can use the warm down to emphasise the importance of working as a team, either with a fun challenge or by offering the opportunity to communicate with teammates within a group or pairs at the end of the practice. The players should be encouraged to reflect upon the activity or their own performance.

drill 97 jog and slide

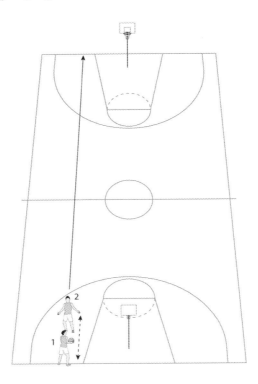

Objective: To improve passing and movement whilst warming down.

Equipment: One ball per pair and the full court.

Description: Player 1 stands on the baseline, facing the court and holding the ball. Player 2 stands 1 m away, on the court and facing player 1. The players pass the ball continually to each other, but progress up the court at jogging speed. Player 1 is moving in a forward direction and player 2 is moving in a backward direction. Once the players reach the far end of the court, they switch roles and repeat the drill. This sequence can continue for five minutes.

Coaching points: The players should be encouraged to execute a correctly weighted pass and stay on their toes when moving up and down the court.

drill 98 lines drill

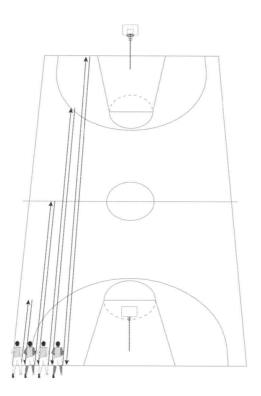

Objective: To warm down by jogging.

Equipment: Team of players and the full court.

Description: The players spread out along the baseline with 1 m between each player. The players begin with a fast jog and run and touch the line that is level with the nearest free throw line and then run back to the baseline; they then run to the halfway line and back; then to the far free throw line and back; and finally to the far baseline and back. The players then repeat this sequence at a medium-paced jog and then again at a slow jog.

Progression: The coach can integrate stretching at various stages of the activity.

Objective: To improve flexibility and warm down after exercise.

Equipment: One ball per player.

Description: The players find a space on the court and stand with their legs slightly wider than shoulder-width apart. The ball is placed on the floor in between the player's legs and is rolled in a figure of eight direction around and in between the legs. The players should slightly bend their knees while also bending their upper body down slowly. After the players have made ten figure of eights, they should walk around before repeating the exercise.

Coaching points: The exercise should be slow and controlled and the players should be encouraged to slightly bend the knees.

drill 100 shooting

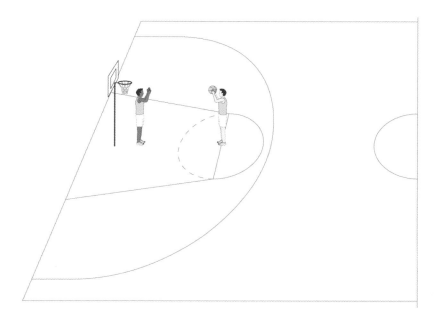

Objective: To improve shooting, whilst warming down.

Equipment: One ball per pair and a basket.

Description: The players are divided into pairs with one shooter and one rebounder. The shooting player takes five shots from the three point line and the partner will rebound and feed the ball after each shot. The players then change roles and once both have completed five shots, both players then stretch. This sequence continues, but on the second round the players shoot from the free throw line and then use a different stretch. On the third round, the players shoot from underneath the basket and again complete a different stretch. The players then walk or jog slowly around the court.

Coaching points: A key focus for this drill should be on warming down, however, the players should still focus upon correct shooting technique and be advised about appropriate stretches.

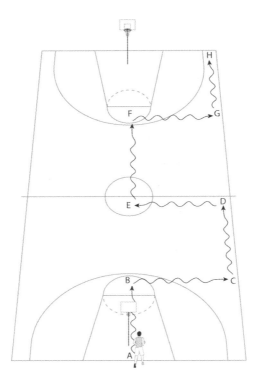

Objective: To warm down and improve footwork.

Equipment: One player, half the court and cones.

Description: The player, holding a ball at point A, jogs with a high knee lift, whilst dribbling the ball to the free throw line at point B. The player then slides to the right (leading with the right foot), whilst dribbling the ball towards C and then jogs with a high knee lift and a dribble to the halfway line at D. The player then dribbles and slides to their left towards E, jogs and dribbles to F and then dribbles and slides to the right to G before finally jogging and dribbling to H. The player then dribbles the ball around the outside of the court and returns to position A. This can be repeated three times with a decrease in speed and the integration of stretching exercises. The coach can involve an entire team in this drill by alternating starting times.

Coaching points: The players should be encouraged to maintain correct posture and defensive stance throughout the drill. The players should be on their toes during the high knee lift action.